THE MINISTRY OF THE SPIRIT

Dr. Adoniram Judson Gordon, the founder of Gordon College of Theology and Missions, has written one of the greatest books on the Holy Spirit that has yet appeared. It combines a deeply devotional examination of Scripture teaching on the subject of the work of the Holy Spirit in this age with a sane and balanced interpretation which provides spiritual blessing and profit to the reader.

This book is a classic, breathing the spiritual vitality of the saintly author and his great contemporaries, Spurgeon, Moody, Meyer, and Maclaren. It remains original in spiritual insight, fertile in suggestiveness, and extremely helpful in its clear presentation of a subject which to many has seemed obscure. This book is well written and should be read and studied with care by pastor, teacher, and layman.

"Dr. Gordon's book on *The Ministry of the Spirit* is so tersely written and so carefully wrought out in every part that there is scarcely one needless noun or heedless adjective.... Every page bristles with new and instructive suggestions; and the whole is so reverent and worshipful that it suggests a man consciously treading on holy ground."

—A. T. P

BETHANY FELLOWSHIP, INC.
Minneapolis, Minnesota

Publishers of
"Books with a Ministry"

The Ministry of
the Spirit

The Ministry of the Spirit

by

A. J. GORDON, D.D.

with

AN INTRODUCTION

by

REV. F. B. MEYER
Formerly Minister at Christ Church, London

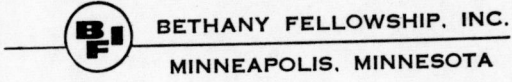

BETHANY FELLOWSHIP, INC.
MINNEAPOLIS, MINNESOTA

This 1964 edition
is reprinted by
Bethany Fellowship, Inc.
by arrangement with
The Judson Press

To the

INHERITORS OF THE SPIRIT

PREFACE

It is not claimed that in this little volume all has been said that might be said upon the subject treated. On the contrary, the writer has proceeded upon the belief that the doctrine of the Holy Spirit can be better understood by limiting the sphere of discussion, rather than by extending it to the largest bounds. For finite beings, at least, presence is more intelligible than omnipresence. So, though the subject of this book is in itself profoundly mysterious, we have sought to simplify it by dwelling upon the time-ministry of the Holy Ghost without entering upon the consideration of his eternal ministry. What the Spirit did before the incarnation of Christ, and what he may do hereafter beyond the second advent of Christ, is a question hardly touched upon in this volume. We have sought rather to emphasize and to magnify the great truth that the Paraclete is now present in the church: that we are living in the dispensation of the Spirit, with all the unspeakable blessing for the church and for the world which this economy provides. Hence, as we speak of the ministry of Christ meaning a service embraced within defined limits, so we name this volume the "Ministry of the Spirit," as referring to the work of the Comforter extending from Pentecost to the end of this dispensation.

How deep a subject for a study! What prayer more becoming for those entering upon it than the humble petition that the Spirit himself will teach us concerning the Spirit! Deeply sensible of the imperfection of this work, it is now committed to the use and blessing of that Divine Person of the Godhead of whom it so unworthily speaks.

A. J. G.

Boston, Dec., 1894.

INTRODUCTION

It is remarkable how many in these last days
have been led to deal with the sublime subject to
which this treatise is devoted. Without doubt the
mind of the church is being instructed, and her
heart prepared for a recognition of the indwelling,
administration, and co-operation of the blessed
Paraclete, which has never been excelled in her history, and is fraught with the greatest promise both
to her and to the world.

Each of these treatises has brought out some
new phase in respect to the person or mission of
the Holy Spirit, but I cannot recall one that is so
lucid, so suggestive, so scriptural, so deeply
spiritual as this, by my beloved friend, Dr. Gordon.
The chapters on the Embodying, the Enduement,
and the Administration of the Spirit seem specially
fresh and helpful. But all is good, and deserving
of prayerful perusal. Let only such truths be well
wrought into the mental and spiritual constitution

of God's servants, and there would be such a revival of pure and undefiled religion in the churches, and such marvelous results through them on the world that the age would close with a world-wide Pentecost. And there are many symptoms abroad that this also is in the purpose of God. Nothing else can meet the deepest needs and yearn ings of our time.

Christianity is beset with three powerful currents, which insidiously operate to deflect her from her course. Materialism, which denies or ignores the supernatural, and concentrates its heed on ameliorating the outward conditions of human life; criticism, which is clever at analysis and dissection, but cannot construct a foundation on which the religious faculty may build and rest; and a fine literary taste, which has greatly developed of late, and is disposed to judge of power by force of words or by delicacy of expression.

To all of these we have but one reply. And that is, not a system, a creed, a church, but the living Christ, who was dead, but is alive forevermore, and has the keys to unlock all perplexities, problems, and failures. Though society could be reconstituted, and material necessities be more evenly supplied, discontent would break out again in some other form, unless the heart were satisfied with his love. The truth which he reveals to the soul, and which is ensphered in him, is alone able to appease the consuming hunger of the mind for data on which to construct its answer to the questions of life and destiny and God, which are ever knocking at its door for solution. And men have yet to learn that the highest power is not in words or metaphors or bursts of eloquence, but in the in-dwelling and out-working of the Word, who is the wisdom and the power of God, and who deals with regions below those where the mind vainly labors.

Jesus Christ, the ever-living Son of God, is the one supreme answer to the restlessness and travail of our day. But he cannot, he will not reveal him-self. Each person in the Holy Trinity reveals another. The Son reveals the Father, but his own revelation awaits the testimony of the Holy Ghost, which, though often given directly, is largely through the church. What we need then, and what the world is waiting for, is the Son of God, borne witness to and revealed in all his radiant beauty of the ministry of the Holy Spirit, as he energizes with and through the saints that make up the holy and mystical body, the church.

It is needful to emphasize this distinction. In some quarters it seems to be supposed that the Holy Spirit himself is the solution of the perplexities of our time. Now what we may witness in some coming age we know not, but in this it is clear that God in the person of Christ is the one only and divine answer. Here is God's yea and amen, the Alpha and Omega, sight for the blind, healing for the paralyzed, cleansing for the polluted, life for the dead, the gospel for the poor and sad and comfortless. Now we covet the gracious bestowal of the Spirit, that he may take more deeply of the things of Christ, and reveal them unto us. When the disciples sought to know the Father, the Lord said, He that hath seen me hath seen the Father. It is his glory that shines on my face, his will that molds my life, his purpose that is fulfilled in my ministry. So the blessed Paraclete would turn our thought and attention from himself to him, with whom he is One in the Holy Trinity, and whom he has come to reveal.

INTRODUCTION

Throughout the so-called Christian centuries the voice of the Holy Spirit has borne witness to the Lord, directly and mediately. Directly, in each widespread quickening of the human conscience, in each revival of religion, in each era of advance in the knowledge of divine truth, in each soul that has been regenerated, comforted, or taught. Mediately his work has been carried on through the church, the body of those that believe. But, alas! how sadly his witness has been weakened and hindered by the medium through which it has come. He has not been able to do many mighty works because of the unbelief which has kept closed and barred those avenues through which he would have poured his glad testimony to the unseen and glorified Lord.

The divisions of the church, her strife about matters of comparative unimportance, her magnification of points of difference, her materialism, her love of pelf and place and power, her accounting herself rich and increased in goods and needing nothing, when she was poor, and miserable, and blind, and naked—these things have not only robbed her of her testimony, but have grieved and

quenched the Holy Spirit, and nullified his testimony.

We gladly hail the signs that this period of
apathy and resistance is coming to a close. The
Church which is in the churches is making herself
felt, is arising from the dust and arraying herself
in her beautiful garments. There is a widespread
recognition of the unity of all who believe, together
with an increasing desire to magnify the points of
agreement and minimize those of divergence. The
great conventions for the quickening of spiritual life
on both sides of the Atlantic in which believers
meet, irrespective of name or sect, are doing an
incalculable amount of good in breaking down the
old lines of demarcation, and making real our
spiritual oneness. The teaching of consecration
and cleanliness of heart and life is removing those
obstacles that have restrained and drowned the
Spirit's still small voice. The fuller's soap and
the refiner's fire have been largely resorted to, with
the best results. And as believers have become
more consistent and devoted, they have grown
increasingly sensitive to the indwelling, energy, and
co-witness of the Holy Spirit.

If only this glorious movement is permitted to achieve its full purpose, the effect will be transcendently glorious. The church will become as pliant to the Divine Tenant as the resurrection body of our Lord to the impulse of his divine nature. And so the Lord Jesus will increasingly become the object of human hope, the center around which the concentric circles of human life shall circle.

That the Lord Jesus should be thus magnified and glorified through the ministry of the Holy Spirit, and with this end in view, that the hearts and lives of believers should be made more sensitive to and receptive of his blessed energy, this treatise has been prepared; and I add my testimony to the beloved author's, that in the mouth of two witnesses, every word may be established; and my prayer to his that the yea of the Spirit to the great voice of the gospel may be heard more mightily and persistently amongst us.

F B Meyer

CONTENTS

CONTENTS

CHAPTER VIII.

CHAPTER IX.

1. Of Sin ; 2. Of Righteousness ; 3. Of Judgment.

CHAPTER X.

I

THE AGE-MISSION OF THE SPIRIT

"It is evident that the present dispensation under which we are is the dispensation of the Spirit, or of the Third Person of the Holy Trinity. To him in the Divine economy, has been committed the office of applying the redemption of the Son to the souls of men by the vocation, justification, and salvation of the elect. We are therefore under the personal guidance of the Third Person, as truly as the apostles were under the guidance of the Second."—*Henry Edward Manning.*

I

THE AGE-MISSION OF THE SPIRIT—INTRODUCTORY

IN some observations on the doctrine of the Spirit, which lie before us as we write, an eminent professor of theology remarks on the disproportionate attention which has been given to the person and work of the Holy Spirit, as compared with that bestowed on the life and ministry of Jesus Christ. It is affirmed, moreover, that in many of the works upon the subject now extant there is a lack of definiteness of impression which leaves much still to be desired in the treatment of this subject. These observations lead us to ask : Why not employ the same method in writing about the Third Person of the Trinity as we use in considering the Second Person ? Scores of excellent lives of Christ have been written ; and we find that in these, almost without exception, the divine story begins with Bethlehem and ends with Olivet Though the Saviour lived before his incarnation, and continues to live after his ascension, yet it gives a certain definiteness of impression to limit one's view to his historic career, distinguishing his visible life lived in time from his invisible life lived in eternity.

So in considering the Holy Spirit, we believe there is an advantage in separating his ministry in time from his ministry before and after, bounding it by Pentecost on the one side, and by Christ's second coming on the other.   We have to confess that in many respects one of the best treatises on the Spirit which we have found is by a Roman Catholic — Cardinal Manning.   Notwithstanding the papistical errors which abound in the volume, his general conception of the subject is in some particulars admirable.   His treatise is called "The Temporal Mission of the Holy Ghost."   How much is suggested by this title!   Just as Jesus Christ had a time-ministry which he came into the world to fulfill, and having accomplished it returned to the Father, so the Holy Spirit, for the fulfillment of a definite mission, came into the world at an appointed time ; he is now carrying on his ministry on earth, and in due time he will complete it and ascend to heaven again—this is what these words suggest, and what, as we believe, the Scriptures teach.   If we thus form a right conception of this present age-ministry of the Spirit, we have a defi nite view-point from which to study his operations in the ages past, and his greater mission, if there be such, in the ages to come.

Now we conceive that the vagueness and mystery attaching in many minds to the doctrine of the Spirit, are due largely to a failure to recognize his time-ministry, distinct from all that went before and introductory to all that is to come after—a ministry with a definite beginning and a definite termination. Certainly no one can read the farewell discourse of our Lord, as recorded by John, without being impressed with the fact that just as distinctly as his own advent was foretold by prophets and angels, he now announces the advent into the world of another, co-equal with himself, his Divine successor, his other self in the mysterious unity of the Godhead. And moreover, it seems clear to us that he implied that this coming One was to appear not only for an appointed work, but for an appointed period: "He shall give you another Comforter, that he may abide with you forever"—εἰς τὸν αἰῶνα. If we translate literally and say "*for the age*," it harmonizes with a parallel passage. In giving the great commission, Jesus says: "And lo, I am with you alway, even *unto the end of the age.*" Here his presence by the Holy Ghost is evidently meant. The perpetuity of that presence is guaranteed, "with you all the days"; and its bound determined, "*unto the end of the age.*" Not that it need be argued that he shall not be here after this dispensation is finished; but that there is such a thing as a temporal mission of the Holy Spirit does seem to be implied. And a full study confirms the view. The present is the dispensation of

the Holy Ghost; the age-work which he inaugu-
rated on the day of Pentecost is now going on, and
it will continue until the Lord Jesus returns from
heaven, when another order will be ushered in and
another dispensational ministry succeed.

In the well-known work of Moberly, on "The
Administration of the Holy Spirit in the Body of
Christ," the author divides the course of redemption
thus far accomplished into these three stages: The
first age, God the Father; the second age, God the
Son; and the third age, God the Holy Ghost.
This distribution seems to be correct, and so does
his remark upon the inauguration of the last of
these periods on the day of Pentecost. "At that
moment," he says, "the third stage of the development [manifestation] of God for the restoration of
the world finally began, never to come to an end or
to be superseded on earth till the restitution of all
things, when the Son of Man shall come again in
the clouds of heaven, in like manner as his disciples
saw him go into heaven." And what shall be the
next period, "the age to come," whose powers they
have already tasted who have been "made partakers
of the Holy Ghost"? This question need not
be answered, as we have done all that is required,
defined the age of the Spirit which constitutes the
field in which our entire discussion lies.

II

THE ADVENT OF THE SPIRIT

"Therefore the Holy Ghost on this day—Pentecost—de scended into the temple of his apostles, which he had prepared for himself, as a shower of sanctification, appearing no more as a transient visitor, but as a perpetual Comforter and as an eternal inhabitant. He came therefore on this day to his disciples, no longer by the grace of visitation and operation, but by the very presence of his majesty."—*Augustine.*

II

THE ADVENT OF THE SPIRIT

"FOR *the Holy Ghost was not yet*," is the more than surprising saying of John when speaking of "the Spirit which they that believe on him should receive." Had not the Spirit been seen descending upon Jesus like a dove at his baptism, and remaining on him? Had he not been the divine agent in creation, and in the illumination and inspiration of the patriarchs and prophets and seers of the old dispensation? How then could John say that he "was not yet given," as the words read in our Common version? The answer to this question furnishes our best point of departure for an intelligent study of the doctrine of the Spirit. Augustine calls the day of Pentecost the "*dies natalis*" of the Holy Ghost; and for the same reason that the day when Mary "brought forth her first-born son" we name "the birthday of Jesus Christ." Yet Jesus had existed before he lay in the cradle at Bethlehem; he was "in the beginning with God"; he was the agent in creation. By him all things were. But on the day of his birth he became incarnate, that in the flesh he might fulfill his great

ministry as the Apostle and High Priest of our confession, manifesting God to men, and making himself an offering for the sins of the world.   Not
until after his birth in Bethlehem was Jesus in the
world in his official capacity, in his divine ministry
as mediator between man and God; and so not till
after the day of Pentecost was the Holy Spirit in
the world in his official sphere, as mediator between
men and Christ.   In the following senses then is
Augustine's saying true, which calls Pentecost "the
birthday of the Spirit":

1. The Holy Spirit, from that time on, took up
his residence on earth.   The Christian church
throughout all this dispensation is the home of the
Spirit as truly as heaven, during this same period,
is the home of Jesus Christ.   This is according to
that sublime word of Jesus, called by one "the
highest promise which can be made to man": "If
a man love me he will keep my words: and my
Father will love him, and we will come unto him,
and make our abode with him" (John 14 : 23).
This promise was fulfilled at Pentecost, and the
first two Persons of the Godhead now hold residence
in the church through the Third.   The Holy Spirit
during the present time is in office on earth; and
all spiritual presence and divine communion of the
Trinity with men are through him.   In other words,
while the Father and the Son are visibly and per-
sonally in heaven, they are invisibly here in the

body of the faithful by the indwelling of the Comforter. So that though we affirm that on the day of Pentecost the Holy Spirit came to dwell upon earth for this entire dispensation, we do not imply that he thereby ceased to be in heaven. Not with God, as with finite man, does arrival in one place necessitate withdrawal from another. Jesus uttered a saying concerning himself so mysterious and seemingly contradictory that many attempts have been made to explain away its literal and obvious meaning: "And no man hath ascended up to heaven but *he that came down from heaven, even the Son of man who is in heaven*"—Christ on earth, and yet in glory; here and there, at the same time, just as a thought which we embody in speech and send forth from the mind, yet remains in the mind as really and distinctly as before it was expressed. Why should this saying concerning our divine Lord seem incredible? And as with the Son, so with the Spirit. The Holy Ghost is here, abiding perpetually in the church; and he is likewise there, in communion with the Father and the Son from whom he proceeds, and from whom, as co-equal partner in the Godhead, he can never be separated any more than the sunbeam can be dissociated from the sun in which it has its source.

2. Again: The Holy Spirit, in a mystical but very real sense, became embodied in the church on the day of Pentecost. Not that we would by any

means put this embodiment on the same plane with
the incarnation of the Second Person of the Trinity.
When "the Word was made flesh and dwelt among
us," it was God entering into union with sinless
humanity; here it is the Holy Spirit uniting himself with the church in its imperfect and militant
condition.   Nevertheless, it is according to literal
Scripture that the body of the faithful (is) indwelt *present tense*
by the divine Spirit.   In this fact we have the distinguishing peculiarity of the present dispensation.
"For he dwelleth with you and *shall be in you*,"
said Jesus, speaking anticipatively of the coming of
the Comforter; and so truly was this prediction fulfilled that ever after the day of Pentecost the Holy
Spirit is spoken of as being in the church.   "*If so
be that the Spirit of God dwell in you*" is the inspired assumption on which the deep teaching in
Romans eighth proceeds.   All the recognition
and deference which the disciples paid to their
Lord they now pay to the Holy Spirit, his true
vicar, his invisible self, present in the body of believers.   How artlessly and naturally this comes out
in the findings of the first council at Jerusalem:
"It seemed good *to the Holy Ghost and to us*" runs
the record; as though it had been said: "Peter and
James and Barnabas and Saul and the rest were
present, and also just as truly was the Holy Ghost."

And when the first capital sin was committed
in the church, in the conspiracy and falsehood

of Ananias and Sapphira, Peter's question is: " Why hath Satan filled thine heart to lie to the Holy Ghost?" "How is it that ye have agreed together to tempt the Holy Ghost?" Not only is the personal presence of the Spirit in the body of believers thus distinctly recognized, but he is there in authority and supremacy, as the center of the assembly. "Incarnated in the church!" do we say? We get this conception by comparing together the inspired characterizations of Christ and of the church. "This temple" was the name which he gave to his own divine person, greatly to the scandal and indignation of the Jews; and the evangelist explains to us that "he spoke of the temple of his body." A metaphor, a type! do we say? No! He said so because it was so. "The Word was made flesh and tabernacled among us, and we beheld his glory" (John 1 : 14). This is temple imagery. "Tabernacled" (ἐσχήνωσεν) is the word used in Scripture for the dwelling of God with men; and the temple is God's dwelling-place. The "glory" harmonizes with the same idea. As the Shechinah cloud rested above the mercy-seat, the symbol and sign of God's presence, so from the Holy of Holies of our blessed Lord's heart did the glory of God shine forth, "the glory as of the only begotten of the Father, full of grace and truth," certifying him to be the veritable temple of the Most High.

After his ascension and the sending down of the

Spirit, the church takes the name her Lord had borne before ; she is the temple of God, and the only temple which he has on earth during the present dispensation. "Know ye not that ye are the temple of God, and that the Spirit of God dwelleth in you?" asks the apostle. This he speaks to the church in its corporate capacity. "A holy temple in the Lord, in whom ye also are *builded together* for a habitation of God through the Spirit," is the sublime description in the Epistle to the Ephesians. It is enough that we now emphasize the fact that the same language is here applied to the church which Christ applies to himself. As with the Head, so with the mystical body ; each is indwelt by the Holy Spirit, and thus is God in some sense incarnated in both ; and for the same reason. Christ was "the Image of the Invisible God"; and when he stood before men in the flesh he could say to them, "He that hath seen me hath seen the Father." Not otherwise than through the incarnation, so far as we know, could the unknown God become known, and the unseen God become seen. So, after Christ had returned to the Father, and the world saw him no more, he sent the Paraclete to be incarnated in his mystical body, the church. As the Father revealed himself through the Son, so the Son by the Holy Spirit now reveals himself through the church ; as Christ was the image of the invisible God, so the church is appointed to be the image of the invisible Christ ; and his members, when they are glorified with him, shall be the express image of his person.

This then is the mystery and the glory of this dispensation ; not less true because mysterious ; not less practical because glorious. In an admirable work on the Spirit, the distinction between the former and the present relation of the Spirit is thus stated : " In the old dispensation the Holy Spirit wrought *upon* believers, but did not in his person dwell in believers and abide permanently in them. He appeared unto men ; he did not incarnate himself in man. His action was intermittent ; he went and came like the dove which Noah sent forth from the ark, and which went to and fro, finding no rest ; while in the new dispensation he dwells, he abides in the heart as the dove, his emblem, which John saw descending and alighting on the head of Jesus. Affianced of the soul, the Spirit went oft to see his betrothed, but was not yet one with her ; the marriage was not consummated until the Pentecost, after the glorification of Jesus Christ." [1]

3. A still more obvious reason why before the day of Pentecost it could be said that " the Holy Ghost was not yet," is contained in the words, "*Because that Jesus was not yet glorified.*" In the order of the unfolding ages we see each of the persons of the Godhead in turn exercising an earthly

---

[1] " The Work of the Holy Spirit in Man," by Pastor Tophel, p. 32.

ministry and dealing with man in the work of redemption.   Under the law, God the Father comes down to earth and speaks to men from the cloud of Sinai and from the glory above the mercy-seat; under grace, God the Son is in the world, teaching, suffering, dying, and rising again; under the dispensation of election and out-gathering now going on, the Holy Spirit is here carrying on the work of renewing and sanctifying the church, which is the body of Christ.   There is a necessary succession in these Divine ministries, both in time and in character.   In the days of Moses it might have been said: "Christ is not yet," because the economy of God-Jehovah was not completed.   The law must first be given, with its sacrifices and types and ceremonies and shadows; man must be put on trial under the law, till the appointed time of his schooling should be completed.   *Then* must Christ come to fulfill all types and terminate all sacrifices in himself; to do for us "what the law could not do in that it was weak through the flesh," and to become "the end of the law for righteousness to every one that believeth."   When in turn Christ had completed his redemption-work by dying on the cross for our sins, and rising again from the dead for our justification, and had taken his place at God's right hand for perpetual intercession, *then* the Holy Ghost came down to communicate and realize to the church the finished work of Christ.

In a word, as God the Son fulfills to men the work of God the Father, so God the Holy Ghost realizes to human hearts the work of God the Son.

There is a holy deference, if we may so say, between the Persons of the Trinity in regard to their respective ministries.   When Christ was in office on earth, the Father commends us to him, speaking from heaven and saying : " This is my beloved Son, hear ye him "; when the Holy Ghost had entered upon his earthly office, Christ commends us to him, speaking again from heaven with sevenfold reiteration, saying : " He that hath an ear, let him hear what *the Spirit* saith unto the churches."[1]   As each Person refers us to the teaching of the other, so in like manner does each in turn consummate the ministry of the other. Christ's words and works were not his own, but his Father's :   " The words which I speak unto you I speak not of myself, but the Father that dwelleth in me he doeth the works." [2]   The Spirit's teaching and communications are not his own, but Christ's : " Howbeit when he the Spirit of truth is come, he will guide you into all truth ; *for he shall not speak of himself; but whatsoever he shall hear that shall he speak ;* and he will show you things to come." " *He shall glorify me ; for he shall receive of mine and show it unto you.*"

This order in the ministries of the Persons ·of

---

[1] See epistles to the seven churches : Rev 2 : 11.   [2] John 14 : 10.

the Godhead is so fixed and eternal that we find it
distinctly foreshadowed even in the typical teaching
of the Old Testament.   Many speak slightingly of
the types, but they are as accurate as mathematics ;
they fix the sequence of events in redemption as
rigidly as the order of sunrise and noontide is fixed
in the heavens.   Nowhere in tabernacle or in temple,
shall we ever find the laver placed before the altar.
The altar is Calvary and the laver is Pentecost ;
one stands for the sacrificial blood, the other for
the sanctifying Spirit.   If any high priest were
ignorantly to approach the brazen laver without
first having come to the brazen altar, we might
expect a rebuking voice to be heard from heaven :
" Not yet the washing of water " ; and such a saying would signify exactly the same as :   " Not yet
the Holy Ghost."

Again, when the leper was to be cleansed,
observe that the blood was to be put upon the tip
of his right ear, the thumb of his right hand, and
the great toe of his right foot ; and then the oil was
to be put upon the right ear, the right thumb, and
the right foot—*the oil upon the blood of the trespass-
offering* (Lev. 14).   Never, we venture to say, in
all the manifold repetitions of this divine ceremony,
was this order once inverted, so that the oil was
first applied, and then the blood ; which means, in-
terpreting type into antitype, that it was impossible
that Pentecost could have preceded Calvary, or

that the outpouring of the Spirit should have anticipated the shedding of the blood.

Then let us reflect, that not only the order of these two great events of redemption was fixed from the beginning, but their dates were marked in the calendar of typical time. The slaying of the paschal lamb told to generation after generation, though they knew it not, the day of the year and week on which Christ our Passover should be sacrificed for us. The presentation of the wave sheaf before the Lord, "*on the morrow after the Sabbath*" [1] had for long centuries fixed the time of our Lord's resurrection on the first day of the week. And the command to "count from the morrow after the Sabbath, from the day that ye brought the sheaf of the wave offering, *seven Sabbaths*," [1] determined the day of Pentecost as the time of the descent of the Spirit. We sometimes think of the disciples waiting for an indefinite period in that upper room for the fulfillment of the promise of the Father; but the time had been fixed not only with God in eternity, but in the calendar of the Hebrew ritual upon earth. They tarried in prayer for ten days, simply because after the forty days of the Lord's sojourn on earth subsequent to his resurrection, ten days remained of the "seven Sabbaths" period.

To sum up what we are saying: The Spirit of God is the successor of the Son of God in his offi-

---

[1] Lev. 23 : 11-16.

cial ministry on earth.   Until Christ's earthly work for his church had been finished, the Spirit's work in this world could not properly begin.   The office of the Holy Ghost is to communicate Christ to us —Christ in his entireness.   However perfectly the photographer's plate has been prepared, there can be no picture until his subject steps into his place and stands before him.   Our Saviour's redemptive work was not completed when he died on the cross, or when he rose from the dead, or even when he ascended from the brow of Olivet.   Not until he sat down in his Father's throne, summing up all his ministry in himself,—" I am he that liveth and was dead, and behold I am alive forevermore,"—did the full Christ stand ready to be communicated to his church.[1]   By the first Adam's sin, God's communion with man through the Holy Ghost was broken, and their union ruptured.   When the second Adam came up from his cross and resurrection, and took his place at God's right hand, there was a restoration of this broken fellowship.   Very beautiful are

---

[1] " Christ having reached his goal, and not till then, bequeathes to his followers the graces that invested his earthly course; the ascending Elijah leaves his mantle behind him.   It is only an extension of the same principle, that the declared office of the Holy Spirit being to complete the image of Christ in every faithful follower by effecting in this world a spiritual death and resurrection,—a point attested in every epistle,—*the image could not be stamped until the reality had been wholly accomplished ; the Divine Artist could not fitly descend to make the copy before the entire original had been provided.*"—*Archer Butler.*

the words of our risen Lord as bearing on this point : " I ascend to my Father and your Father, to my God and your God." [1] The place which the divine Son had won for himself in the Father's heart, he had won for us also. All of acceptance and standing and privilege which was now his, was ours too, by redemptive right ; and the Holy Ghost is sent down to confirm and realize to us what he had won for us. Without the expiatory work of Christ for us, the sanctifying work of the Spirit in us were impossible ; and on the other hand, without the work of the Spirit within us, the work of Christ for us were without avail.

" *And when the day of Pentecost was fully come.*" What these words mean historically, typically, and doctrinally, we are now prepared to see. The true wave sheaf had been presented in the temple on high. Christ the first-fruits, brought from the grave on " the morrow after the Sabbath," or the first day of the week, now stands before God accepted on our behalf ; the seven Sabbaths from the resurrection day have been counted, and Pentecost has come. Then suddenly, to those who were " all of one accord in one place," " there came a sound from heaven as of a rushing mighty wind, and it filled all

---

[1] John 20 : 17. " Because though he and the Father are one, and the Father his Father by the propriety of nature, to us God became a Father through the Son, not by right of nature, but by grace."—*Ambrose.*

the house where they were sitting, and there appeared unto them cloven tongues, like as of fire, and sat upon each of them, and they were all filled with the Holy Ghost." As the manger of Bethlehem was the cradle of the Son of God, so was the upper room the cradle of the Spirit of God; as the advent of "the Holy Child" was a testimony that God had "visited and redeemed his people," so was the coming of the Holy Ghost. The fact that the Comforter is here, is proof that the Advocate is there in the presence of the Father. Boldly Peter and the other apostles now confront the rulers with their testimony, "Whom ye slew and hanged on a tree . . . Him hath God exalted with his right hand to be a prince and a Saviour, to give repentance to Israel and forgiveness of sins; and we are his witnesses of these things; *and so also is the Holy Ghost, whom God hath given to them that obey him.*" As the sound of the golden bells upon the high priest's garments within the Holiest gave evidence that he was alive, so the sound of the Holy Ghost, proceeding from heaven and heard in that upper chamber, was an incontestable witness that the great High Priest whom they had just seen passing through the cloud-curtain, entering within the veil, was still living for them in the presence of the Father. Thus has the "*dies natalis*," the birthday of the Holy Spirit, come; and the events of his earthly mission will now be considered in their order.

III

THE NAMING OF THE SPIRIT

"The name Paraclete is applied to Christ as well as to the Spirit; and properly: For it is the common office of each to console and encourage us and to preserve us by their defense. Christ was their [the disciples'] patron so long as he lived in the world; he then committed them to the guidance and protection of the Spirit. If any one asks us whether we are not under the guidance of Christ, the answer is easy: Christ is a perpetual guardian, but not visibly. As long as he walked on the earth he appeared openly as their guardian: now he preserves us by his Spirit. He calls the Spirit 'another Comforter,' in view of the distinction which we observe in the blessings proceeding from each."—*John Calvin.*

III

THE NAMING OF THE SPIRIT

THE Son of God was named by the angel before he was conceived in the womb: "Thou shalt call his name Jesus, for he shall save his people from their sins." Thus he came, not to receive a name, but to fulfill a name already predetermined for him. In like manner was the Holy Ghost named by our Lord before his advent into the world: "But when the Paraclete is come, whom I will send unto you from the Father" (John 15: 26). This designation of the Holy Spirit here occurs for the first time—a new name for the new ministry upon which he is now about to enter. The reader will find in almost any critical commentary discussions of the meaning of the word, and of the question of its right translation, whether by "Comforter," or "Advocate," or "Teacher," or "Helper." But the question cannot be fully settled by an appeal to classical or patristic Greek, for the reason, we believe, that it is a divinely given name whose real significance must be made manifest in the actual life and history of the Spirit. The name is the person himself, and only as we know the person can we interpret his name. Why attempt then to translate this word any more than we do the name of Jesus? We might well transfer it into our English version, leaving the history of the church from the Acts of the Apostles to the experience of the latest saint to fill into it the great significance which it was intended to contain. Certain it is that the language of the Holy Ghost can never be fully understood by an appeal to the lexicon. The heart of the church is the best dictionary of the Spirit. While all the before-mentioned synonyms are correct, neither one is adequate, nor are all together sufficient to bring out the full significance of this great name, "The Paraclete."

Let us consider, however, how much is suggested by the literal meaning of this word, "the *Paracletos*," and by all that our Lord says concerning him in his last discourse. "To call to one's aid," is the meaning of the verb, παρακαλέω, from which the name is derived. Very beautiful therefore is the word in its application to the disciples of Christ at the time when the Spirit was given. They had lost the visible presence of their Lord. The sorrow of his removal from them through the cross and the sepulchre had after three days been turned into joy by his resurrection. But now another separation had come, in his departure to the Father after the cloud had received him out of sight. In this last and longer bereavement, what should they do? Their beloved Master had told them beforehand

what to do.   They were to call upon the Father to
send them One to fill the vacant place, and he who
should be sent would be the " Paraclete," the " one
called to their help." [1]

But what deep questionings must have arisen in
their hearts as they heard the Saviour's promise :
" If I go not away the Paraclete will not come unto
you; but if I depart I will send him unto you."
Did they begin to ask whether the mysterious
comer would be a " person " ? Impossible to
imagine. For he was to take the place of that
greatest of persons ; to do for them even greater
things than he had done ; and to lead them into
even larger knowledge than he had imparted.
The discussion of the personality of the Holy
Ghost is so unnatural in the light of Christ's
last discourse that we studiously avoid it.   Let us
treat the question, therefore, from the point of view
of Christ's own words, and try to put ourselves
under the impression which they make upon us.
To state the matter as simply and familiarly as possible : Jesus is about to vacate his office on earth as
teacher and prophet ; but before doing so he would
introduce us to his successor.   As in a complex
problem we seek to determine an unknown quantity
by the known, so in this paschal discourse Jesus

---

[1] The word παρακλήτωρ is used in the Septuagint (Job 16 : 2) with
the meaning of "*Comforter*," and the term παράκλητος occurs in the
Talmud, signifying "*Interpreter*."

aims to make us acquainted with the mysterious, invisible coming personage whom he names the "Paraclete" by comparing him with himself, the known and the visible one. Collating his comparisons we may find in them several groups of seeming contradictions, and just such contradictions as we should expect if this comer is indeed a person of the Godhead. Of the coming Paraclete then we find these intimations.[1]

1. He is another, yet the same : "And I will pray the Father and he shall give you another Comforter" (John 14 : 16). By the use of this expression "another" our Lord distinguishes the Paraclete from himself, but he also puts him on the same plane with himself. For there is no parity or even comparison between a person and an influence. If the promised visitor were to be only an impersonal emanation from God, it would seem impossible that our Lord should have so co-ordinated him with himself as to say : "I go to be an Advocate for you in heaven (1 John 2 : 1), and I send another to be an Advocate for you on earth."

---

[1] The most obvious reason for concluding that the Holy Spirit is a person is that he performs actions and stands in relations which belong only to a person, *e. g.*: *He speaks* (Acts 1 : 16); *he works miracles* (Acts 2 : 4; 8 : 39); *he sets ministers over churches* (Acts 20: 28); *he commands and forbids* (Acts 8 : 29; 11 : 12; 13 : 2; 16 : 6, 7); *he prays for us* (Rom. 8 : 26); *he witnesses* (Rom. 8 : 16); *he can be grieved* (Eph. 4 : 30); *he can be blasphemed* (Mark 3 : 29); *he can be resisted* (Acts 7 : 51, etc).

But if Christ thus distinguishes the Comforter from himself, he also identifies him with himself: "I will not leave you orphans: *I will come to you*" (John 14 : 18). By common consent this promise refers to the advent of the Spirit, for so the connection plainly indicates. And yet almost in the same breath he says: "The Comforter whom I will send unto you" (John 14 : 26). Thus our Lord makes the same event to be at once his coming and his sending; and he speaks of the Spirit now as his own presence, and now as his substitute during his absence. So what must we conclude but that the Paraclete is Christ's other self, a third Person in that blessed Trinity of which he is the second.

2. The Paraclete is subordinate yet superior in his ministry to the church. "For he shall not speak of himself; but whatsoever he shall hear that shall he speak   He shall glorify me; for he shall receive of mine and show it unto you" (John 16 : 13). Well may we mark the holy deference between the persons of the Trinity which is here pointed out. Each receives from another what he communicates, and each magnifies another in his praises. As Bengel concisely states it: "The Son glorifies the Father; the Spirit glorifies the Son." What then is the office of the Holy Ghost, so far as we can interpret it, but that of communicating and applying the work of Christ to human hearts? If he convinces of sin it is by exhibiting the

gracious redemptive work of the Saviour and showing men their guilt in not believing on him. If he
witnesses to the penitent of his acceptance it is by
testifying of the atoning blood of Jesus in which
that acceptance is grounded; if he regenerates and
sanctifies the heart it is by communicating to it the
life of the risen Lord. Christ is "all" in himself,
and through the Spirit "in all" those whom the
Spirit renews. This reverent subjection of the
earthly Comforter to the heavenly Christ contains
a deep lesson for those who are indwelt by the
Spirit [1] and makes them rejoice evermore to be
witnesses rather than originators.

With this subordination of the Holy Spirit to
Christ, how is it yet true that such a great advantage was to accrue to the church by the departure
of the Saviour and the consequent advent of the
Spirit to take his place? That it would be so is what
is plainly affirmed in the following text: "Nevertheless I tell you the truth. It is expedient for you
that I go away: for if I go not away the Comforter
will not come unto you; but if I depart I will send
him unto you" (John 16 : 7). If the Spirit is simply
the measure of the Son, his sole work being to communicate the work of the Son, what gain could
there be in the departure of the one in order to

---

[1] If the Holy Spirit may not speak of himself as preacher, how
canst thou draw thy preaching out of thyself—out of thine head or
even out of thine heart.—*Pastor Gossner*.

the coming of the other? Would it not be simply the exchange of Christ for Christ?—his visible presence for his invisible?

To us the answer of this question is most obvious. It was not the earthly Christ whom the Holy Ghost was to communicate to the church, but the heavenly Christ,—the Christ re-invested with his eternal power, re-clothed with the glory which he had with the Father before the world was, and re-endowed with the infinite treasures of grace which he had purchased by his death on the cross. It is as though—to use a very inadequate illustration—a beloved father were to say to his family: "My children, I have provided well for your needs; but your condition is one of poverty compared with what it may become. By the death of a kinsman in my native country I have become heir to an immense estate. If you will only submit cheerfully to my leaving you and crossing the sea, and entering into my inheritance, I will send you back a thousand times more than you could have by my remaining with you." Only in the instance we are considering, Christ is the "testator" as well as the heir. By his death the inheritance becomes available, and when he had ascended into heaven he sent down the Holy Spirit to distribute the estate among those who were joint heirs with him. What this estate is, may be best summarized in two beautiful expressions of frequent recurrence in the

epistles of Paul, " The riches of his grace " (Eph. 1 :
7), and " The riches of his glory " (Eph. 3 : 16).   On
the cross " the riches of his grace " was secured to
us in the forgiveness of sins ; on the throne " the
riches of his glory " was secured to us in our being
strengthened with all might by his Spirit in the
inner man ; in the indwelling of Christ in our
hearts by faith, and in our infilling with all the fullness of God.   The divine wealth only becomes
completely available on the death, resurrection, and
ascension of our Lord ; so that the Holy Spirit, the
divine Conveyancer, had not the full inheritance to
convey till Jesus was glorified.

Observe therefore, in the valedictory discourse
of our Lord, the frequent recurrence of the words :
" *Because I go to the Father*," one of the sayings
which greatly perplexed his disciples.   In the light
of all which Jesus says in this connection, let us
see if its meaning may not be clear to us.   " If ye
loved me ye would rejoice because I go unto the
Father ; for the Father is greater than I " (John
14 : 28), he says in the same connection.   We cannot here enter into the deep question of the *kenosis*,
or self-emptying of the Son of God in his incarnation.   It is enough that we follow the plain teaching of the Scripture, that though " being in the
form of God, he counted it not a thing to be
grasped to be on an equality with God ; but emptied
himself, taking the form of a servant " (Phil. 2 :

6, 7, R. V.). What now does his going to the Father signify but a refilling with that of which he had been emptied, or a resumption of his co-equality with God? The greater blessing which he could confer upon his church by his departure seems to lie in the fact of the greater power and glory into which he would enter by his enthronement at God's right hand As Luther pointedly puts it : "Therefore do I go, he saith, where I shall be greater than I now am, that is, to the Father, and it is better that I shall pass out of this obscurity and weakness into the power and glory in which the Father is." In the light of this interpretation the meaning of our Lord's words above quoted does not seem difficult. The Paraclete was to communicate Christ to his church,—his life, his power, his riches, his glory. In his exaltation all these were to be very greatly increased. "All things that the Father hath are mine" (John 16 : 15), he says. And though he had for a time voluntarily disinherited himself of his heavenly possessions, he is now to be repossessed of them. "Therefore said I, that he shall take of mine and shall show it unto you" (16 : 15). Christ at God's right hand will have more to give than while on earth ; therefore the church will have more to receive through the Paraclete than through the visible Christ. What obvious significance then do the following sayings from this farewell sermon of Jesus have : "Verily

verily, I say unto you, He that believeth on me the works that I do shall he do also; greater works than these shall he do; *because I go unto the Father*" (John 14 : 12). The earthly Christ is equal only to himself thus conditioned; and if the Holy Spirit shall communicate his power to his disciples, they will do the same works that he does. But the heavenly Christ is co-equal with the Father, therefore when he shall ascend to the Father, and the Spirit shall take of his and communicate to his church, it will do greater works than these. The stream of life, in other words, will have greater power because of the higher source from which it proceeds. Very deep are the mysteries here considered, and we can only speak of them in the light which we get by comparing Scripture with Scripture. Did the risen Christ breathe on his disciples and say to them : " Receive ye the Holy Ghost " ? [1] "It is enough, Lord, that we have received the Spirit from thee," they might well have said. Yet it was not enough for him to give; for looking on to the day of his enthronement, he says : " But when the Paraclete is come, whom I will send unto you from the Father, even the Spirit of truth which proceedeth from the Father, he shall testify of me " (John 15 : 26). When Jesus hath ascended " on high," then can the

---

[1] Let it be observed that in this communication of the risen Christ it is not said, " Receive ye *the* Holy Ghost "—the article being significantly omitted—Λάβετε Πνεῦμα ἅγιον (John 20 : 22).

Holy Ghost communicate "the power from on high." Therefore it is expedient that he go away.

As with the power which Christ was to impart to his church through the Paraclete, so with the righteousness which he was both to impute and to impart ; its highest source must be found in heaven : " And when he, the Comforter, is come, he will convince the world of righteousness ; . . . of righteousness *because I go to my father*, and ye see me no more " (John 16 : 8–10). We may say truly that the righteousness of Christ was not completely finished and authenticated till he sat down at the right hand of the majesty on high. By his death he perfectly satisfied the claims of a violated law, but this fact was not attested until the grave gave back the certificate of discharge in his released and risen body. By his resurrection he was " declared to be the Son of God in power, according to the Spirit of holiness " (Rom. 1 : 4). But the fact was not fully verified till God had " set him at his own right hand in the heavenly places, far above all principality, and power, and might, and dominion, and every name that is named " (Eph. 1 : 20, 21). Now in his consummated glory he is prepared to be " made wisdom, and righteousness, and sanctification, and redemption " to his people. He who had been " manifest in the flesh " that he might be made sin for us, was now " justified in the Spirit " and " received up into glory," that he might be made righteousness to us, and that "we might be made the righteousness of God in him." Christ's coronation, in a word, is the indispensable condition to our justification. Till he who was made a curse for us is crowned with glory and honor we cannot be assured of our acceptance with the Father.[1] How deep the current of thought which flows through this narrow channel—"Because I go to the Father."

3. The Paraclete teaches only the things of Christ; yet teaches more than Christ taught: "I have yet many things to say unto you, but ye cannot bear them now. Howbeit when he the Spirit of truth is come, he will guide you into all the truth" (John 16 : 12, 13). It is as though he had said: "I have brought you a little way in the knowledge of my doctrine; he shall bring you all the way." One reason for this saying seems plain: The teaching of Jesus during his earthly ministry waited to be illumined by a light not risen—the light of the cross, the light of the sepulchre, the light of the ascension. Therefore until these events had come to pass, Christian doctrine was undeveloped, and could not be fully communicated to the disciples of Christ. But this is not all. The "because I go to the Father" still gives the key to our Lord's meaning. "But what things so-

---

[1] How righteous must he be, who will go to the Father from the cross and the grave! Thus will the Holy Spirit convince the world that he is a righteous man, and truly righteous for man.—*Roos.*

ever he shall hear, these shall he speak, and he shall declare unto you things to come" (John 16 : 13, R. V.). Very wonderful is this hint of the mutual converse of the Godhead, so that the Paraclete is described as listening while he leads, as having an ear in heaven attentive to the converse of the Father and the glorified Son, while he extends an unseen guidance to the flock on earth, communicating to them what he has heard from the Father and the Son. And we may reverently ask, Has not the glorified Christ more of knowledge and revelation to communicate than he had in the days of his humiliation? Of "the things to come" has he not secrets to impart which hitherto may have been hidden in the counsels of the Father? To take a single illustration from the words of Christ. Speaking of his second advent, he says : " But of that day or that hour knoweth no one, not even the angels in heaven, neither the Son, but the Father" (Mark 13 : 32[1]). It is best that we should interpret these words frankly, and instead of saying, with some, that he did not know in the sense that he was not permitted to disclose, admit it possible that while in his humiliation and under the veil of his incarnation, this secret was hidden from his eyes.

But is it not presumptuous for us to reason, that

---

[1] " Neither the Son " : " It is more than *neither;* it is *not yet the Son,*" says Morrison the commentator.

therefore he does not *now* know the day of his coming? How constantly is that text quoted as a decisive and final prohibition of all inquiry into the proximate time of our Lord's return in glory. But they who so use this saying simply remand us to the childhood of the church, to the spiritual nonage of the ante-Pentecostal days. Have we forgotten that since our Lord ascended to the Father he has given us a further revelation, that wondrous book of the Apocalypse, which opens and closes with a beatitude upon those who read and faithfully keep the words of this prophecy? And one characteristic feature of this book is its chronological predictions concerning the time of the end, its mystical dates, which have led many sober searchers of the word of God to inquire diligently "what and what manner of time" the Spirit did signify in giving us these way-marks in the wilderness. This being so, we may ask: If we are not irreverent in concluding with many devout expositors that our Saviour meant what he said in declaring that he did "not yet" know the time of his advent, are we presumptuous in taking literally the opening words of the Apocalypse?: "The Revelation of Jesus Christ, which God gave unto him, to show unto his servants the things which must shortly come to pass." It was because of his going unto the Father that greater works and greater riches were to attend the church after Pentecost. Why may we not assign to the same cause also the fuller revelation of the future and the leading into completer truth concerning the blessed hope of the church? In other words, if we may think of Christ as entering into larger revelation as he returns to the glory which he had with the Father must we not think of larger communications of truth by the blessed Paraclete?

Have we not learned something of the nature and offices of the Spirit by this study of his new name, and of all that the departing Lord says in the wondrous discourse wherein he introduces him to his disciples? At least the study should enable us to distinguish two inspired terms which have been needlessly confounded by not a few writers, viz.: the words "*Paraclete*," and "*Parousia*." The latter word, which constantly occurs in Scripture as describing our Lord's second coming, has been applied in several learned works to the advent of the Holy Spirit; and since Christ came in the person of the Spirit, it has been argued that the Redeemer's promised advent in glory has already taken place. But this is to confuse terms whose use in Scripture marks them as clearly distinct. Observe their difference: In the Paraclete, Christ comes spiritually and invisibly; in the Parousia, he comes bodily and gloriously. The advent of the Paraclete is really conditioned on the Saviour's personal departure from his people: "If I go not away the Paraclete will not come to you" (John 16 : 7).

The Parousia, on the other hand, is only realized in his personal return to his people : " For what is our hope or joy or crown of rejoicing ? Are not even ye in the *presence* of our Lord Jesus Christ *at his coming*?" (1 Thess. 2 : 19.)   The Paraclete attends the church in the days of her humiliation ; the Parousia introduces the church into the day of her glory.   In the Paraclete, Christ came to dwell with the church on earth : " I will not leave you orphans ; I will come to you" (John 14 : 18).   In the Parousia, Christ comes to take the church to dwell with himself in glory : " I will come again and receive you unto myself ; that where I am there ye may be also" (John 14 : 3).   Christ prayed on behalf of his bereaved church for the coming of this Paraclete : " And I will pray the Father and he shall give you another Paraclete."   The Holy Spirit now prays with the pilgrim-church for the hastening of the Parousia.   " And the Spirit and the bride say, Come " (Rev. 22 : 17).   These two can only be understood in their mutual relations.   Christ, who gave the new name to the Holy Spirit, can best interpret that name to us by making us acquainted with himself.   May that name be for us so real a symbol of personal presence that while strangers and pilgrims in the earth we may walk evermore " in the *paraclesis* of the Holy Ghost" (Acts 9 : 31).

IV

THE EMBODYING OF THE SPIRIT

"But now the Holy Ghost is given more perfectly, for he is no longer present by his operation as of old, but is present with us so to speak, and converses with us in a substantial manner. For it was fitting that, as the Son had conversed with us in the body, the spirit should also come among us in a bodily manner."—*Gregory Nazianzen.*

IV

THE EMBODYING OF THE SPIRIT

"THE church, which is his body," began its history and development at Pentecost. Believers had been saved, and the influences of the Spirit had been manifested to men in all previous dispensations from Adam to Christ. But now an *ecclesia*, an outgathering, was to be made to constitute the mystical body of Christ, incorporated into him the Head and indwelt by him through the Holy Ghost. The definition which we sometimes hear, that a church is "a voluntary association of believers, united together for the purposes of worship and edification" is most inadequate, not to say incorrect. It is no more true than that hands and feet and eyes and ears are voluntarily united in the human body for the purposes of locomotion and work. The church is formed from within; Christ present by the Holy Ghost, regenerating men by the sovereign action of the Spirit, and organizing them into himself as the living center. The Head and the body are therefore one, and predestined to the same history of humiliation and glory. And as they are one in fact, so are they one in name. He whom God anointed and filled with the Holy Ghost

53

is called "the Christ," and the church, which is his body and fullness, is also called "the Christ." "For as the body is one, and hath many members, and all the members of that one body, being many, are one body, *so also is the Christ*" (I Cor. 12 : 12). Here plainly and with wondrous honor the church is named ὁ Χριστός, commenting upon which fact Bishop Andrews beautifully says : "Christ is both in heaven and on earth ; as he is called the Head of his church, he is in heaven ; but in respect of his body which is called Christ, he is on earth."

So soon as the Holy Ghost was sent down from heaven this great work of his embodying began, and it is to continue until the number of the elect shall be accomplished, or unto the end of the present dispensation.   Christ, if we may say it reverently, became mystically a babe again on the day of Pentecost, and the hundred and twenty were his infantile body, as once more through the Holy Ghost he incarnated himself in his flesh.   Now he is growing and increasing in his members, and so will he continue to do "till we all come in the unity of the faith and of the knowledge of the Son of God unto a perfect man, unto the measure of the stature of fullness of Christ."   Then the Christ on earth will be taken up into visible union with the Christ in heaven, and the Head and the body be glorified together.   Observe how the history of the church's formation, as recorded in the Acts, harmonizes with the conception given above. The story of Pentecost culminates in the words, "and the same day there were added about three thousand souls" (Acts 2 : 41). Added to whom? we naturally ask. And the King James translators have answered our question by inserting in italics "to them." But not so speaks the Holy Ghost. And when, a few verses further on in the same chapter, we read: "And the Lord added to the church daily such as should be saved," we need to be reminded that the words "to the church" are spurious. All such glosses and interpolations have only tended to mar the sublime teaching of this first chapter of the Holy Spirit's history. "And believers were the more added *to the Lord*" (Acts 5 : 14.) "And much people were added *unto the Lord*" (Acts 11 : 24.) This is the language of inspiration—Not the mutual union of believers, but their divine co-uniting with Christ; not voluntary association of Christians, but their sovereign incorporation into the Head and this incorporation effected by the Head through the Holy Ghost.

If we ask concerning the way of admission into this divine *ecclesia*, the teaching of Scripture is explicit: "For in one Spirit were we all baptized into one body" (1 Cor. 12 : 13). The baptism in water marks the formal introduction of the believer into the church; but this is the symbol, not the substance. For observe the identity of form between the ritual

and the spiritual. "I indeed baptize you in water,"
. . said John, "but he that cometh after me . . .
shall baptize you in the Holy Ghost and in fire"
(Matt. 3 : 11). As in the one instance the disciple
was submerged in the element of water, so in the
other he was to be submerged in the element of the
Spirit. And thus it was in actual historic fact. The
upper room became the Spirit's baptistery, if we may
use the figure. His presence "filled all the house
where they were sitting," and "they were all filled
with the Holy Ghost." The baptistery would never
need to be re-filled, for Pentecost was once and for
all, and the Spirit then came to abide in the church
perpetually. But each believer throughout the age
would need to be infilled with that Spirit which
dwells in the body of Christ. In other words, it
seems clear that the baptism of the Spirit was given
once for the whole church, extending from Pentecost to Parousia. "There is one Lord, one faith,
one baptism" (Eph. 4 : 5). As there is one body
reaching through the entire dispensation, so there is
"one baptism" for that body given on the day of
Pentecost. Thus if we rightly understand the meaning of Scripture it is true, both as to time and as to
fact, that "in one Spirit we were all baptized into one
body, whether Jews or Greeks, whether bond or free."

The typical foreshadowing, as seen in the church
in the wilderness, is very suggestive at this point:
"Moreover, brethren, I would not that ye should be

ignorant, how that all our fathers were under the cloud and all passed through the sea; and were all baptized unto Moses in the cloud and in the sea" (1 Cor. 10 : 1). Baptized *into* Moses by their passage through the sea, identified with him as their leader, and committed to him in corporate fellowship; even so were they also baptized into Jehovah, who in the cloud of glory now took his place in the midst of the camp and tabernacled henceforth with them. The type is perfect as all inspired types are. The antitype first appears in Christ our Lord, baptized in water at the Jordan, and then baptized in the Holy Ghost which "descended from heaven like a dove and abode upon him." Then it recurred again in the waiting disciples, who besides the baptism of water, which had doubtless already been received, now were baptized "in the Holy Ghost and in fire." Henceforth they were in the divine element, as their fathers had been in the wilderness, "not in the flesh but *in the Spirit*" (Rom. 8 : 9); called "to live according to God *in the Spirit*" (1 Peter 4 : 6); to "walk *in the Spirit*" (Gal. 5 : 25); "praying always with all prayer and supplication *in the Spirit*" (Eph. 6 : 18). In a word, on the day of Pentecost the entire body of Christ was baptized into the element and presence of the Holy Ghost as a permanent condition. And though one might object that the body as a whole was not yet in existence, we reply that neither was the complete church in ex-

istence when Christ died on Calvary, yet all believers are repeatedly said to have died with him.

To change the figure of baptism for a moment to
another which is used synonymously, that of the
anointing of the Spirit, we have in Exodus a beautiful typical illustration of our thought.   At Aaron's
consecration the precious ointment was not only
poured upon his head, but ran down in rich profusion upon his body and upon his priestly garments.
This fact is taken up by the psalmist when he sings:
"Behold how good and pleasant it is for brethren to
dwell together in unity.   It is like the precious
ointment upon the head that ran down upon the
beard, even Aaron's beard, that went down to the
skirts of his garments" (Ps. 133 : 1, 2).   Of our
great High Priest we read: "How God anointed
Jesus of Nazareth with the Holy Ghost and with
power" (Acts 10 : 38).   But it was not for himself
alone but also for his brethren that he obtained this
holy unction.   He received that he might communicate.   "Upon whom thou shalt see the Spirit descending and remaining on him, the same is he that baptizeth in the Holy Ghost" (John 1 : 33).   And now
we behold our Aaron, our great High Priest, who has
passed through the heavens, Jesus the Son of God,
standing in the holiest in heaven.   "Thou didst
love righteousness and didst hate iniquity," is the
divine encomium now passed upon him, "therefore
God, thy God, anointed thee with the oil of gladness

above thy fellows" (Heb. 1 : 9).   He, the *Christos*, the Anointed, stands above and for the *Christoi*, his anointed brethren, and from him the Head, the unction of the Holy Ghost descended on the day of Pentecost.   It was poured in rich profusion upon his mystical body.   It has been flowing down ever since, and will continue to do so till the last member shall have been incorporated with himself, and so anointed by the one Spirit into the one body, which is the church.

It is true that in one instance subsequent to Pentecost the baptism in the Holy Ghost is spoken of.   When the Spirit fell on the house of Cornelius, Peter is reminded of the word of the Lord, how that he said : "John indeed baptized in water, but ye shall be baptized in the Holy Ghost " (Acts 11 : 16). This was a great crisis in the history of the church, the opening of the door of faith to the Gentiles, and it would seem that these new subjects of grace now came into participation of an already present Spirit. Yet Pentecost still appears to have been the age-baptism of the church.   As Calvary was once for all, so was the visitation of the upper room.

Consider now that, as through the Holy Ghost we become incorporated into the body of Christ, we are in the same way assimilated to the Head of that body, which is Christ.   An unsanctified church dishonors the Lord, especially by its incongruity. A noble head, lofty-browed and intellectual, upon a

deformed and stunted body, is a pitiable sight.
What, to the angels and principalities who gaze,
evermore upon the face of Jesus, must be the sight
of an unholy and misshapen church on earth,
standing in that place of honor called "his body."
Photographing in a sentence the *ecclesia* of the
earliest centuries, Professor Harnack says: "*Originally the church was the heavenly bride of Christ,
and the abiding place of the Holy Spirit.*" Let the
reader consider how much is involved in this definition. The first and most sacred relation of the
body is to the head. Watching for the return of
the Bridegroom induces holiness of life and conduct in the bride; and the supreme work of the
Spirit is directed to this end, that "He may establish our hearts unblamable in holiness before God
our Father, at the coming of our Lord Jesus Christ
with all his saints" (1 Thess. 3 : 13). In accomplishing this end he effects all other and subordinate ends. The glorified Christ manifests himself
to man through his body. If there is a perfect
correspondence between himself and his members,
then there will be a true manifestation of himself
to the world.[1] Therefore does the Spirit abide in
the body, that the body may be "inChristed," to

---

[1] "The Holy Spirit not only dwells in the church as his habitation,
but also uses her as the living organism whereby he moves and walks
forth in the world, and speaks to the world and acts upon the world.
He is the soul of the church which is Christ's body."—*Bishop Webb,
The Presence and Office of the Spirit, p. 47.*

use an old phrase of the mystics; that is, indwelt by Christ and transfigured into the likeness of Christ. Only thus, as "a chosen generation, a royal priesthood, a holy nation, a peculiar people," can it "shew forth the virtues of him who has called us out of darkness into his marvelous light." And who is the Christ that is thus to be manifested? From the throne he gives us his name: "I am he that liveth and was dead, and behold I am alive for evermore" (Rev. 1 : 18). Christ in glory is not simply what he is, but what he was and what he is to be. As a tree gathers up into itself all the growths of former years, and contains them in its trunk, so Jesus on the throne is all that he was and is and is to be. In other words, his death is a perpetual fact as well as his life.

And his church is predestined to be like him in this respect, since it not only heads up in him, as saith the apostle, that ye "may grow up into him in all things which is the Head, even Christ," but also bodies itself forth from him, "from whom the whole body, fitly joined together and compacted by that which every joint supplieth, . . maketh increase of the body" . . (Eph. 4 : 16). If the church will literally manifest Christ, then she must be both a living and a dying church. To this she is committed in the divinely given form of her baptism. "Know ye not that so many of us as were baptized into Jesus Christ were baptized into his death; therefore we were buried with him by baptism into death, that like as Christ was raised up from the dead by the glory of the Father, even so we also should walk in newness of life" (Rom. 6 : 3, 4). And the baptism of the Holy Ghost into which we have been brought is designed to accomplish inwardly and spiritually what the baptism of water foreshadows outwardly and typically, viz., to reproduce in us the living and the dying of our Lord.

First, the living. "For the law of the Spirit of life in Christ Jesus hath made me free from the law of sin and death" (Rom. 8 : 2). That is, that which has been hitherto the actuating principle within us, viz., sin and death, is now to be met and mastered by another principle, the law of life, of which the Holy Spirit of God is the author and sustainer. As by our natural spirit we are connected with the first Adam, and made partakers of his fallen nature, so by the Holy Spirit we are now united with the second Adam, and made partakers of his glorified nature. To vivify the body of Christ by maintaining its identity with the risen Head is, in a word, the unceasing work of the Holy Ghost.

Secondly, the dying of our Lord in his members is to be constantly effected by the indwelling Spirit. The church, which is the fullness of him that filleth all in all," completes in the world his crucifixion as well as his resurrection. This is certainly Paul's profound thought, when he speaks of filling up "that which is behind of the afflictions of Christ in my flesh, for his body's sake, which is the church" (Col. 1 : 24). In other words, the church, as the complement of her Lord, must have a life experience and a death experience running parallel.

It is remarkable how exact is this figure of the body, which is employed to symbolize the church. In the human system life and death are constantly working together. A certain amount of tissue must die every day and be cast out and buried, and a certain amount of new tissue must also be created and nourished daily in the same body. Arrest the death-process, and it is just as certain to produce disorder as though you were to arrest the life-process. Literally is this true of the corporate body also. The church must die daily in fulfillment of the crucified life of her Head, as well as live daily in the manifestation of his glorified life. This italicised sentence, which we take from a recent book, is worthy to be made a golden text for Christians : "*The Church is Christian no more than as it is the organ of the continuous passion of Christ.*" To sympathize, in the literal sense of suffering with our sinning and lost humanity, is not only the duty of the church, but the absolutely essential condition to her true manifestation of her Lord. A self-indulgent church disfigures Christ; an avaricious church bears false witness against Christ; a worldly church betrays Christ, and gives him over once more to be mocked and reviled by his enemies.

The resurrection of our Lord is prolonged in his body, as we all see plainly. Every regeneration is a pulse-beat of his throne-life. But too little do we recognize the fact that his crucifixion must be prolonged side by side with his resurrection. "If any man will come after me let him deny himself and take up his cross daily and follow me." The church is called to live a glorified life in communion with her Head, and a crucified life in her contact with the world. And the Holy Spirit dwells evermore in the church to effect this twofold manifestation of Christ. "But God be thanked, that ye have obeyed from the heart that pattern of doctrine to which ye were delivered," writes the apostle (Rom. 6 : 17). The pattern, as the context shows, is Christ dead and risen. If the church truly lives in the Spirit, he will keep her so plastic that she will obey this divine mold as the metal conforms to the die in which it is struck. If she yields to the sway of "the spirit that now worketh in the children of disobedience," she will be stereotyped according to the fashion of the world, and they that look upon her will fail to see Christ in her.

V

THE ENDUEMENT OF THE SPIRIT

"To the disciples, the baptism of the Spirit was very distinctly not his first bestowal for regeneration, but the definite communication of his presence in power of their glorified Lord. Just as there was a two-fold operation of the one Spirit in the Old and New Testaments, of which the state of the disciples before and after Pentecost was the striking illustration, so there may be, and in the great majority of Christians is, a corresponding difference of experience. . . When once the distinct recognition of what the indwelling of the Spirit was meant to bring is brought home to the soul, and it is ready to give up all to be made partaker of it, the believer may ask and expect what may be termed a baptism of the Spirit. Praying to the Father in accordance to the two prayers in Ephesians, and coming to Jesus in the renewed surrender of faith and obedience, he may receive such an inflow of the Holy Spirit as shall consciously lift him to a different level from the one on which he has hitherto lived."
—*Rev. Andrew Murray.*

V

THE ENDUEMENT OF THE SPIRIT

WE have maintained in the previous chapter that the baptism in the Holy Ghost was given once for all on the day of Pentecost, when the Paraclete came in person to make his abode in the church. <u>It does not follow therefore that every believer has received this baptism.</u> <u>God's gift is one thing ; our appropriation of that gift is quite another thing.</u> Our relation to the second and to the third persons of the Godhead is exactly parallel in this respect. " God so loved the world that he *gave* his only begotten Son " (John 3 : 16). " But as many as *received him* to them gave he the right to become the children of God, even to them that believe on his name" (John 1 : 12). Here are the two sides of salvation, the divine and the human, which are absolutely co-essential.

There is a doctrine somewhat in vogue, not inappropriately denominated redemption by incarnation, which maintains that since God gave his Son to the world, all the world has the Son, consciously or unconsciously, and that therefore all the world will be saved. It need not be said that a true evangelical teaching must reject this theory as utterly untenable, since it ignores the necessity of individual faith in Christ. But some orthodox writers have urged an almost identical view with respect to the Holy Ghost. They have contended that the enduement of the Spirit is "not any special or more advanced experience, but simply the condition of every one who is a child of God"; that "believers converted after Pentecost, and living in other localities, are just as really endowed with the indwelling Spirit as those who actually partook of the Pentecostal blessing at Jerusalem."[1]

On the contrary, it seems clear from the Scriptures that it is still the duty and privilege of believers to receive the Holy Spirit by a conscious, definite act of appropriating faith, just as they received Jesus Christ. We base this conclusion on several grounds. Presumably if the Paraclete is a person, coming down at a certain definite time to make his abode in the church, for guiding, teaching, and sanctifying the body of Christ, there is the same reason for our accepting him for his special ministry as for accepting the Lord Jesus for his special ministry. To say that in receiving Christ we necessarily received in the same act the gift of the Spirit, seems to confound what the Scriptures make distinct.[2] For it is as sinners that we accept

---

[1] Rev. E. Boys, " Filled with the Spirit," p. 87.

[2] It is assumed by some that because those that walked with Christ of old received the baptism of the Holy Ghost and fire at Pentecost,

Christ for our justification, but it is as sons that we accept the Spirit for our sanctification: "And because ye are sons, God hath sent forth the Spirit of his Son into your hearts, crying Abba, Father" (Gal. 4 : 6).   Thus, when Peter preached his first sermon to the multitude after the Spirit had been given, he said: "Repent and be baptized, every one of you, in the name of Jesus Christ, for the remission of sins, and ye shall receive the gift of the Holy Ghost" (Acts 2 : 38).

This passage shows that logically and chronologically the gift of the Spirit is subsequent to repentance.   Whether it follows as a necessary and inseparable consequence, as might seem, we shall consider later.   Suffice that this point is clear, so clear that one of the most conservative as well as ablest writers on this subject, in commenting on this text in Acts, says: "Therefore it is evident that the reception of the Holy Ghost, as here spoken of, has nothing whatever to do with bringing men to believe and repent.   It is a subsequent operation; it is an additional and

---

more than eighteen hundred years ago, therefore all believers now have received the same.   As well might the apostles, when first called, have concluded that because at his baptism the Spirit like a dove rested upon Christ, therefore they had equally received the same blessing.   Surely the Spirit has been given and the work in Christ wrought for all; but to enter into possession, to be enlightened and made partakers of the Holy Ghost, there must be a personal application to the Lord, etc.—*Andrew Jukes*, " *The New Man.*"

separate blessing; it is a privilege founded on faith already actively working in the heart. . . I do not mean to deny that the gift of the Holy Ghost may be practically on the same occasion, but never in the same moment. The reason is quite simple too. The gift of the Holy Ghost *is grounded on the fact that we are sons by faith in Christ, believers resting on redemption in him.* Plainly, therefore, it appears that the Spirit of God has already regenerated us."[1]

Now, as we examine the Scriptures on this point, we shall see that we are required to appropriate the Spirit as sons, in the same way that we appropriated Christ as sinners. "As many as received him, even to them that believe on his name," is the condition of becoming sons, as we have already seen, receiving and believing being used as equivalent terms. In a kind of foretaste of Pentecost, the risen Christ, standing in the midst of his disciples, "breathed on them and said, Receive ye the Holy Ghost." The verb is not passive, as our English version might lead us to suppose, but has here as generally an active signification, just as in the familiar passage in Revelation : "Whosoever will, let him *take* the water of life freely." Twice in the Epistle to the Galatians the possession of the Holy Ghost is put on the same grounds of active appro-

---

[1] William Kelly, " Lectures on the New Testament Doctrine of the Holy Spirit," p. 161.

priation through faith : "Received ye the Spirit by the works of the law or by the hearing of faith?" (3 : 2). "That ye might receive the promise of the Spirit through faith" (3 : 14). These texts seem to imply that just as there is a "faith toward our Lord Jesus Christ" for salvation, there is a faith toward the Holy Ghost for power and consecration.

If we turn from New Testament teaching to New Testament example we are strongly confirmed in this impression. We begin with that striking incident in the nineteenth chapter of Acts. Paul, having found certain disciples at Ephesus, said unto them : "Did ye receive the Holy Ghost when ye believed? And they said unto him, Nay ; we did not so much as hear whether there is a Holy Ghost." This passage seems decisive as showing that one may be a disciple without having entered into possession of the Spirit as God's gift to believers. Some admit this, who yet deny any possible application of the incident to our own times, alleging that it is the miraculous gifts of the Spirit which are here under consideration, since, after recording that when Paul had laid his hands upon them and "the Holy Ghost came upon them," it is added that "they spake with tongues and prophesied." All that need be said upon this point is simply that these Ephesian disciples, by the reception of the Spirit, came into the same condition with the upper-room disciples who received him some twenty years before, and of whom it is written that "they were all filled with the Holy Ghost and began to speak with other tongues as the Spirit gave them utterance." In other words, these Ephesian disciples on receiving the Holy Ghost exhibited the traits of the Spirit common to the other disciples of the apostolic age.

Whether those traits—the speaking of tongues and the working of miracles—were intended to be perpetual or not we do not here discuss. But that the presence of the personal Holy Spirit in the church was intended to be perpetual there can be no question. And whatsoever relations believers held to that Spirit in the beginning they have a right to claim to-day. We must withhold our consent from the inconsistent exegesis which would make the water baptism of the apostolic times still rigidly binding, but would relegate the baptism in the Spirit to a bygone dispensation. We hold indeed, that Pentecost was once for all, but equally that the appropriation of the Spirit by believers is always for all, and that the shutting up of certain great blessings of the Holy Ghost within that ideal realm called "the apostolic age," however conve nient it may be as an escape from fancied difficulties, may be the means of robbing believers of some of their most precious covenant rights.[1]   Let us trans-

---

[1] It is a great mistake into which some have fallen, to suppose that the results of Pentecost were chiefly miraculous and temporary

fer this incident of the Ephesian Christians to our own times.   We need not bring forward an imaginary case, for by the testimony of many experienced witnesses the same condition is constantly encountered.   Not only individual Christians, but whole communities of disciples are found who have been so imperfectly instructed that they have never known that there is a Holy Spirit, except as an influence, an impersonal something to be vaguely recognized.   Of the Holy Ghost as a Divine Person, dwelling in the church, to be honored and invoked and obeyed and implicitly trusted, they know nothing.   Is it conceivable that there could be any deep spiritual life or any real sanctified energy for service in a community like this?   And what should a well-instructed teacher or evangelist do, on discovering a church or an individual Christian in such a condition?   Let us turn to another passage of the Acts for an answer : " Now when the apostles which were at Jerusalem heard that Samaria had received the word of God they sent unto them Peter and John, who when they were come down prayed for them that they might receive the Holy Ghost ; for as yet he had fallen upon none of them ; only they were baptized in the name

---

The effect of such a view is to keep spiritual influences out of sight ; and it will be well ever to hold fast the assurance that a wide, deep, and perpetual spiritual blessing in the church is that which above all things else was secured by the descent of the Spirit after Christ was glorified.—*Dr. J. Elder Cumming, "Through the Eternal Spirit."*

of the Lord Jesus. Then laid they their hands on them and they received the Holy Ghost " (Acts 8 : 14–17).

Here were believers who had been baptized in water. But this was not enough. The baptism in the Spirit, already bestowed at Pentecost, must be appropriated. Hear the prayer of the apostles "that they might receive the Holy Ghost." Such prayer we deem eminently proper for those who to-day may be ignorant of the Comforter. And yet such prayer should be followed by an act of believing acceptance on the part of the willing disciple : " O Holy Spirit, I yield to thee now in humble surrender. I receive thee as my Teacher, my Comforter, my Sanctifier, and my Guide." Do not testimonies abound on every hand of new lives resulting from such an act of consecration as this, lives full of peace and power and victory among those who before had received the forgiveness of sins but not the enduement of power ?

We conceive that the great end for which the enduement of the Spirit is bestowed is our qualification for the highest and most effective service in the church of Christ. Other effects will certainly attend the blessing, a fixed assurance of our acceptance in Christ, and a holy separateness from the world ; but these results will be conducive to the greatest and supreme end, our consecrated usefulness.

Let us observe that Christ, who is our example in this as in all things, did not enter upon his ministry till he had received the Holy Ghost. Not only so, but we see that all his service from his baptism to his ascension was wrought in the Spirit. Ask concerning his miracles, and we hear him saying: "I by the Spirit of God cast out devils" (Matt. 12 : 28). Ask concerning that decease which he accomplished at Jerusalem, and we read "that he through the eternal Spirit offered himself without spot unto God" (Heb. 9 : 14). Ask concerning the giving of the great commission, and we read that he was received up "after that he through the Holy Ghost had given commandments unto the apostles" (Acts 1 : 2). Thus, though he was the Son of God, he acted ever in supreme reliance upon him who has been called the "Executive of the Godhead."

Plainly we see how Christ was our pattern and exemplar in his relation to the Holy Spirit. He had been begotten of the Holy Ghost in the womb of the virgin, and had lived that holy and obedient life which this divine nativity would imply. But when he would enter upon his public ministry, he waited for the Spirit to come upon him, as he had hitherto been in him. For this anointing we find him praying: "Jesus also being baptized and praying, the heaven was opened, and the Holy Ghost descended in a bodily shape like a

dove upon him" (Luke 3 : 22). Had he any
"promise of the Father" to plead, as he now asked
the anointing of the Spirit, if as we may believe
this was the subject of his prayer? Yes; it had
been written in the prophets concerning the rod out
of the stem of Jesse: "And the Spirit of the
Lord shall rest upon him; the spirit of wisdom and
understanding, the spirit of counsel and might,
the spirit of knowledge and of the fear of the
Lord" (Isa. 11 : 2). "The promise of the sevenfold Spirit," the Jewish commentators call it. Certainly it was literally fulfilled upon the Son of God
at the Jordan, when God gave him the Spirit without measure. For he who was now baptized was
in turn to be baptizer. "Upon whom thou shalt
see the Spirit descending, and remaining on him,
the same is he which baptizeth with the Holy Ghost"
(John 1 : 33). "I indeed baptize you in water unto
repentance : but he that cometh after me is might-
ier than I . . . he shall baptize you in the Holy
Ghost and in fire" (Matt. 3 : 11, R. V.). And
now being at the right hand exalted, and having "the seven spirits of God" (Rev. 3 : 3), the
fullness of the Holy Ghost, he will shed forth his
power upon those who pray for it, even as the
Father shed it forth upon himself.

Let us observe now the symbols and descriptions
of the enduement of the Spirit which are applied
equally to Christ and to the disciples of Christ.

1. *The Sealing of the Spirit.* We hear Jesus saying to the multitude that sought him for the loaves and fishes, " Labor not for the meat which perisheth, but for that meat which endureth unto eternal life, which the Son of man shall give unto you, *for him hath God the Father sealed*" (John 6 : 27). This sealing must evidently refer back to his reception of the Spirit at the Jordan. One of the most instructive writers on the Hebrew worship and ritual tells us that it was the custom for the priest to whom the service pertained, having selected a lamb from the flock, to inspect it with the most minute scrutiny, in order to discover if it was without physical defect, and then to seal it with the temple seal, thus certifying that it was fit for sacrifice and for food. Behold the Lamb of God presenting himself for inspection at the Jordan ! Under the Father's omniscient scrutiny he is found to be " a lamb without blemish and without spot." From the opening heaven God gives witness to the fact in the words : " This is my beloved Son in whom I am well pleased," and then he puts the Holy Ghost upon him, the testimony to his sonship, the seal of his separation unto sacrifice and service.

The disciple is as his Lord in this experience " In whom having also believed ye were sealed with the Holy Spirit of promise " (Eph. 1 : 13). As always in the statements of Scripture, this transaction is represented as subsequent to faith. It is not conversion, but something done upon a converted soul, a kind of crown of consecration put upon his faith. Indeed the two events stand in marked contrast. In conversion the believer receives the testimony of God and "sets his seal to it that God is true" (John 3 : 33). In consecration God sets his seal upon the believer that he is true. The last is God's "Amen" to the Christian, verifying the Christian's "Amen" to God. "Now he which establisheth us with you in Christ, and anointed us, is God; *who also sealed us* and gave us the earnest of the Spirit in our hearts" (2 Cor. 1 : 21, 22).

If we ask to what we are committed and separated by this divine transaction, we may learn by studying the church's monograph, if such we may name what is brought out in a mysterious passage in one of the pastoral epistles. In spite of the defection and unbelief of some, the apostle says : "Nevertheless the foundation of God standeth sure, having this seal." Then he gives us the two inscriptions on the seal: "The Lord knoweth them that are his"; and, "Let every one that nameth the name of the Lord depart from unrighteousness" (2 Tim. 2 : 19)—Ownership and holiness. When we receive the gift of the Holy Spirit it is that we may count ourselves henceforth and altogether Christ's. If any shrink from this devotement, how can he have the fullness of the Spirit? God cannot put his signature upon what is not his. Hence, if under the sway of a worldly spirit we withhold ourselves from God and insist on self-ownership, we need not count it strange if God withholds himself from us and denies us the seal of divine ownership. God is very jealous of his divine signet. He graciously bestows it upon those who are ready to devote themselves utterly and irrevocably to his service, but he strenuously withholds it from those who, while professing his name, are yet "serving divers lusts and pleasures." There is a suggestive passage in the Gospel of John which, translated so as to bring out the antitheses which it contains, reads thus: "Many trusted in his name, beholding the signs which he did; but Jesus did not trust himself to them" (John 2:23, 24). Here is the great essential to our having the seal of the Spirit. Can the Lord trust us? Nay; the question is more serious. Can he trust himself to us? The Holy Spirit, which is his signet ring, can he commit it to our use for signing our prayers and for certifying ourselves, and his honor not be compromised?

The other inscription on the seal is: "Let every one that nameth the name of the Lord depart from unrighteousness."[1] The possession of the Spirit

---

[1] It will be observed that the inscription on the seal is substantially the same as that upon the forehead of the High Priest, קֹדֶשׁ לַיהוָה —HOLINESS TO THE LORD (Exod. 39:30).

commits us irrevocably to separation from sin. For what is holiness but an emanation of the Spirit of holiness who dwells within us? A sanctified life is therefore the print or impression of his seal: "He can never own us without his mark, the stamp of holiness. The devil's stamp is none of God's badge. Our spiritual extraction from him is but pretended unless we do things worthy of so illustrious birth and becoming the honor of so great a Father." The great office of the Spirit in the present economy is to communicate Christ to his church which is his body. And what is so truly essential of Christ as holiness? "In him is no sin; whosoever abideth in him sinneth not." The body can only be sinless by uninterrupted communion with the Head; the Head will not maintain communion with the body except it be holy.

The idea of ownership, just considered, comes out still further in the words of the apostle: "And grieve not the Spirit of God in whom ye were sealed unto the day of redemption" (Eph. 4 : 30). The day of redemption is at the advent of our Lord in glory, when he shall raise the dead and translate the living. Now his own are in the world, but the world knows them not. But he has put his mark and secret sign upon them, by which he shall recognize them at his coming. In that great quickening, at the Redeemer's advent, the Holy Spirit will be the seal by which the saints will be recognized,

and the power through which they will be drawn up
to God. "If the Spirit that raised up Jesus dwell
in you" (Rom. 11 : 9), is the great condition of final
quickening. As the magnet attracts the particles
of iron and attaches them to itself by first impart-
ing its own magnetism to them, so Christ, having
given his Spirit to his own, will draw them to himself through the Spirit. We are not questioning
now that all who have eternal life dwelling in them
will share in the redemption of the body; we are
simply entering into the apostle's exhortation against
grieving the Spirit. We must fear lest we mar the
seal by which we were stamped, lest we deface or
obscure the signature by which we are to be recognized in the day of redemption.[1]

In a word the sealing is the Spirit himself, now
received by faith and resting upon the believer, with
all the results in assurance, in joy, and in empower-

[1] The allusion to the seal as a pledge of purchase would be pecu-
liarly intelligible to the Ephesians, for Ephesus was a maritime city,
and an extensive trade in timber was carried on there by the ship-
masters of the neighboring ports. The method of purchase was this :
The merchant, after selecting his timber, stamped it with his own
signet, which was an acknowledged sign of ownership. He often did
not carry off his possession at the time; it was left in the harbor with
other floats of timber ; but it was chosen, bought, and stamped ; and
in due time the merchant sent a trusty agent with the signet, who
finding that timber which bore a corresponding impress, claimed and
brought it away for the master's use. Thus the Holy Spirit impresses
on the soul now the image of Jesus Christ; and this is the sure pledge
of the everlasting inheritance.—*E. H. Bickersteth*, " *The Spirit of
Life*," *p. 176*.

ing for service, which must follow his unhindered sway in the soul. Dr. John Owen, who has written more intelligently and more exhaustively on this subject than any with whom we are acquainted, thus sums up the subject : " If we can learn aright how Christ was sealed, we shall learn how we are sealed. The sealing of Christ by the Father is the communication of the Holy Spirit in fullness to him, authorizing him unto and acting his divine power in all the acts and duties of his office, so as to evidence the presence of God with him and approbation of him. God's sealing of believers then is his gracious communication of the Holy Spirit unto them so to act his divine power in them as to enable them unto all the duties of their holy calling, evidencing them to be accepted with him both for themselves and others, and asserting their preservation unto eternal life." [1]

2. *The Fullness of the Spirit.*   Immediately upon his baptism we read : " And Jesus, full of the Holy Spirit, returned from the Jordan and was led by the Spirit into the wilderness " (Luke 4 : 1).   The same record is made concerning the upper-room disciples, immediately after the descent of the Spirit : " And they were all filled with the Holy Spirit " (Acts 2 : 4).   What is here spoken of seems nothing different from what in other Scriptures is

---

[1] John Owen, D. D., " Discourse Concerning the Spirit," pp. 406, 407.

called the reception of the Spirit. It is a transaction that may be repeated, and will be if we are living in the Spirit. But <u>it is clearly an experience</u> <u>belonging to one who has already been converted.</u> This comes out very plainly in the life of Paul. If according to the opinion quoted in the early part of this chapter, the reception of the Spirit is associated always and inseparably with conversion, one will reasonably ask, why a conversion so marked and so radical as that of the apostle to the Gentiles need be followed by such an experience as that named in Acts 9 : 17 : "And Ananias departed and entered into the house, and laying his hands on him, said : Brother Saul, the Lord, even Jesus who appeared unto thee in the way which thou camest, hath sent me that thou mightest receive thy sight and be filled with the Holy Ghost." <u>We seem to have a</u> <u>clear allusion here to that which so constantly ap-</u> <u>pears in Scripture, both in doctrine and in life, a</u> <u>divine something distinct from conversion and sub-</u> <u>sequent to it, which we have called the reception of</u> <u>the Spirit</u>. "The enduement of power" we may well name it ; for observe how constantly throughout the book of Acts mighty works and mighty utterances are connected with this qualification. "Then Peter, *filled with the Holy Ghost*, said unto them" (Acts 4 : 8), is the preface to one of the apostle's most powerful sermons. "And they were *all filled with the Holy Ghost*, and they spake the

word with boldness" (Acts 4 : 31), is a similar
record.   And they chose Stephen, a man *full* of
faith and *of the Holy Ghost*, the narrative runs, regarding the choice of deacons in Acts 6 : 5. "And
he, being *full of the Holy Ghost*," is the keynote to
his great martyr-sermon. This infilling of the Spirit
marks a decisive and most important crisis in the
Christian life, judging from the story of the apostle's
conversion, to which we have just referred.

But, as we have intimated, we are far from maintaining that this is an experience once for all, as the
sealing seems to be. As the words "regeneration"
and "renewal" used in Scripture mark respectively
the impartation of the divine life as a perpetual
possession and its increase by repeated communications, so in our sealing there is a reception of the
Spirit once for all, which reception may be followed
by repeated fillings.   It is reasonable to conclude
this since our capacity is ever increasing and our
need constantly recurring, according to the beautiful saying of Godet : "Man is a vessel destined to
receive God, a vessel which must be enlarged in
proportion as it is filled and filled in proportion as
it is enlarged."

And yet we confess here to a degree of uncer
tainty as to the use of terms, and as to whether
the two now under consideration are identical.
We may well pause therefore and lift a prayer,
that since "we have received not the spirit of

the world but the Spirit which is of God, that we might know the things which are freely given to us of God," this blessed Revelator and Interpreter may not only reveal to us our privilege and inheritance in the Holy Ghost, but teach us to name and dis tinguish the terms by which it is conveyed.

While the fact of which we are speaking seems undoubted, the exposition of it is far from being easy. Therefore we should attach no little value to a consensus of opinion on this subject from those who have thought most carefully and searched most prayerfully concerning it. This is our apology for the multiplied quotations which we are introducing into this chapter, believing that the Holy Spirit is most likely to interpret himself through those who most honor him in seeking his guidance and illumination.

In a recent work upon this subject, in which care· ful scholarship and spiritual insight seem to be well united, the author thus states his conclusions : " It seems to me beyond question, as a matter of experience both of Christians in the present day and of the early church, as recorded by inspiration, that in addition to the gift of the Spirit received at conversion, there is another blessing corresponding in its signs and effects to the blessing received by the apostles at Pentecost—a blessing to be asked for and expected by Christians still, and to be described in language similar to that employed

in the book of the Acts. Whatever that blessing
may be, it is in immediate connection with the
Holy Ghost; and one of the terms by which we
may designate it is 'to be filled with the Spirit.'
As with the early Christians so with us now, the
filling comes when there is special need for it. . .
And there is an occasion when that blessing comes
to a man for the first time. That first time is a
spiritual crisis from which his future spiritual life
must be dated. There may be a question as to
what it is to be called, or at least by what name in
Scripture we are authorized to call it. . . Whether
consciously or not, it is to the fact of the Holy
Spirit's coming in new power to the soul that all
new life is due; and the more that this is consciously
understood the more is the Holy Ghost in his due
place in our hearts. It is only when he is consciously accepted in all his power that we can be
said to be either 'baptized' or 'filled' with the
Holy Ghost. I should like to add that it is possible to maintain that God from the first offered to
his own people a higher position in this matter
than they have generally been able to occupy, in
that the fullness of the Spirit was and is offered to
each soul at conversion; and that it is only from
want of faith that subsequent outpourings of the
Holy Ghost become needful." [1]

---

[1] "Through the Eternal Spirit," by James Elder Cumming, D.D.,
pp. 146, 147.

That the filling of the Spirit belongs to us as a covenant privilege seems to be clear from the exhortation in the Epistle to the Ephesians, which is confessedly of universal application: "Be not drunken with wine, wherein is excess, but be filled with the Spirit" (Eph. 5 : 18). The passive verb employed here is suggestive. The surrendered will, the yielded body, the emptied heart, are the great requisites to his incoming. And when he has come and filled the believer, the result is a kind of passive activity, as of one wrought upon and controlled rather than of one directing his own efforts. Under the influence of strong drink there is an outpouring of all that the evil spirit inspires—frivolity, profanity, and riotous conduct. "Be God-intoxicated men," the apostle would seem to say; "let the Spirit of God so control you that you shall pour yourself out in psalms and hymns and spiritual songs." If such divine enthusiasm has its perils, we believe that they are less to be dreaded than that "moderatism" which makes the servants of God satisfied with the letter of Scripture if only that letter be skillfully and scientifically handled, rather than giving the supreme place to the Spirit as the inspirer and motor of all Christian service.

3. *The Anointing of the Spirit.* After the baptism and temptation we find our Lord appropriating to himself the words of the prophet, as he read them in the synagogue of Nazareth :

" The Spirit of the Lord is upon me, because he hath anointed me to preach good tidings to the poor " (Luke 4 : 18).   Twice in the Acts there is a reference to this important event in similar terms : " Thy holy servant Jesus, whom thou didst anoint " (Acts 4 : 27, R. V.).   " Jesus of Nazareth, how that God anointed him with the Holy Ghost and with power " (Acts 10 : 38).   And as with the Lord so with his disciples : " Now he that establisheth us with you in Christ, and anointed us, is God " (2 Cor. 1 : 21, R. V.).

A student of the Scriptures need not be told how closely the ceremony of anointing was related to all important offices and ministries of the servants of Jehovah under the old covenant.   The priest was anointed that he might be holy unto the Lord (Lev. 8 : 12).   The king was anointed that the Spirit of the Lord might rest upon him in power (1 Sam. 16 : 15).   The prophet was anointed that he might be the oracle of God to the people (1 Kings 19 : 16).   No servant of Jehovah was deemed qualified for his ministry without this holy sanctifying touch laid upon him.   Even in the cleansing of the leper this ceremony was not wanting.   The priest was required to dip his right finger in the oil that was in his left hand and to put it upon the tip of the right ear, upon the thumb of the right hand, and upon the great toe of the right foot of him that was to be cleansed, the oil " *upon*

the blood of the trespass-offering " (Lev. 14 : 17).
Thus with divine accuracy did even the types foretell
the two-fold provision for the Christian life, cleansing
by the blood and hallowing by the oil—justification in Christ, sanctification in the Spirit.

If we ask now what this anointing is, the reply
is obviously the Holy Spirit himself. As before he
was the seal attesting us, so now he is the oil sanctifying us—the same gift described by different
symbols. And as it was the Aaron who had been
the first anointed who was qualified to anoint others,
so with our great High Priest. It is he within the
veil who gives the Spirit unto his own, that he may
qualify them to be "an elect race, a royal priesthood, a holy nation, a people for God's own possession (1 Peter 2 : 9, R. V.). "But ye have an
anointing from the Holy One, and ye know all
things " (1 John 2 : 20). Christ in the New Testament is constantly called "the Holy One." And
because the Spirit was sent to communicate him to
the people, they are made partakers of his knowledge as well as of his holiness. If it should be said
that this unction of which John speaks is miracu
lous, the divine illumination of evangelists and
prophets who were commissioned to be the vehicles
of inspired Scripture, we must call attention to other
passages which connect the knowledge of God with
the Holy Ghost. "For who among men knoweth
the things of a man save the spirit of a man which

is in him ; even so the things of God none knoweth
save the Spirit of God " (1 Cor. 2 : 11, R. V.). The
horse and his rider may see the same magnifi-
cent piece of statuary in the park ; the one may be
delighted with it as a work of human genius, but
upon the dull eye of the other it makes no impression,
and for the reason that it takes a human mind to
appreciate the work of the human mind.   Likewise
only the Spirit of God can know and make known
the thoughts and teachings and revelations of God.
This seems to be the meaning of John in his discourse concerning the divine unction : " But the
anointing which ye have received of him abideth
in you, and ye need not that any man teach you ;
but as the same anointing teacheth you of all things "
(1 John 2 : 27).

In nothing does the enduement of the Spirit
more distinctly manifest itself than in the fine dis-
cernment of revealed truth which it imparts.   As
in service, the contrast between working in the
power of the Spirit and in the energy of the flesh
is easily discernible, even more clearly in knowledge
and teaching is the contrast between the tuition of
learning and the intuition of the Spirit.   While we
should not undervalue the former, it is striking to
note how the Bible puts the weightier emphasis on
the latter ; so that really the unspiritual hearer is
to be accounted less blameworthy for not discerning the truth than the intellectual preacher is for

expecting him to do so.   When, for example, one
attempts with the utmost learning to convince an
unbeliever of the deity of Christ and fails, the
word of Scripture to him is :   " No man is able to
say ' Lord Jesus ' save in the Holy Ghost " (1 Cor.
12 : 3).

The Spirit of Jesus can alone reveal to men
the lordship of Jesus, and this key of knowledge
the Holy Ghost will never put into the hand of
any man however learned.   As it is written that
Christ is the " raying forth " of the Father's glory,
and " the express image of his person " (Heb. 1 : 3),
thus by a beautiful figure reminding us that as we
can only see the sun in the rays of the sun, so we
can only know God in Jesus Christ, who is the
manifestation of God.   It is so likewise between
the second and third Persons of the Trinity.   Christ
is the image of the invisible God; the Holy
Ghost is the invisible image of Christ.   As Jesus
manifested the Father outwardly, the Spirit manifests Jesus inwardly, forming him within us as
the hidden man of the heart, imaging him to the
spirit by an interior impression which no intel
lectual instruction, however diligent, can effect.

In his profound discourse concerning the " unction " and accompanying illumination, John was
only expounding by the Spirit what Jesus had said
before his departure: " Howbeit, when he the
Spirit of truth is come, he will guide you into all

truth; he shall glorify me; for he shall receive of mine and shall show it unto you" (John 16 : 13). "The Spirit of truth"—How much instruction and suggestion is conveyed by this term! As he is called "the Spirit of Christ," as revealing Christ in his suffering and glory, so he is called "the Spirit of truth," as manifesting the truth in all its depths and heights. As impossible as it is that we should know the person of Christ without the Spirit of Christ who reveals him, so impossible it is that we should know the truth as it is in Jesus without the Spirit of truth who is appointed to convey it. "The Spirit of truth whom the world cannot receive" (John 14 : 17)—We must come to Christ before the Spirit can come to us. "The Spirit of truth which proceedeth from the Father" (John 15 : 26)—He can only teach us in intelligent sonship to cry "Abba, Father." The Spirit of truth . . . shall guide you into all truth" (John 16 : 13). Divine knowledge is all and altogether in his power to communicate, and without his illumination it must be hidden from our under-standing.

Thus we have had the enduement of the Spirit presented to us under three aspects—sealing, filling, and anointing—all of which terms, so far as we can understand, signify the same thing—the gift of the Holy Ghost appropriated through faith. Each of these terms is connected with some special

Divine endowment—the seal with assurance and consecration; the filling with power; and the anointing with knowledge. All these gifts are wrapt up in the one gift in which they are included, and without whom we are excluded from their possession.

While thus we conclude that it is a Christian's privilege and duty to claim a distinct anointing of the Spirit to qualify him for his work, we would be careful not to prescribe any stereotyped exercises through which one must necessarily pass in order to possess it. It is easy to cite cases of decisive, vivid, and clearly marked experience of the Spirit's enduement, as in the lives of Dr. Finney, James Brainard Taylor, and many others. And instead of discrediting these experiences—so definite as to time and so distinct as to accompanying credentials—we would ask the reader to study them, and observe the remarkable effects which followed in the ministry of those who enjoyed them. The lives of many of the co-laborers with Wesley and Whitefield give a striking confirmation of the doctrine which we are defending. Years of barren ministry, in which the gospel was preached with orthodox correctness and literary finish, followed, after the Holy Spirit had been recognized and appropriated, by evangelistic pastorates of the most fervent type, such is the history of not a few of these mighty men of God.

Let not this great subject be embarrassed by too minute theological definitions on the one hand, nor by the too exacting demand for striking spiritual exercises on the other, lest we put upon simple souls a burden greater than they can bear.   Nevertheless we cannot emphasize too strongly the divine crisis in the soul which a full reception of the Holy Ghost may bring.   "My little children, of whom I travail in birth again until Christ be formed in you" (Gal. 4 : 19), writes the apostle to those who had already believed on the Son of God.   Whatever he may have meant in this fervent saying, we doubt not that the deepest yearning of the Spirit is for the informing of Christ in the heart, in order to that outward conformity to Christ which is the supreme end of Christian nurture.   If we conceive of the Christian life as only a gradual growth in grace, is there not danger that we come to regard this growth as both invisible and inevitable, and so take little responsibility for its accomplishment?   Let the believer receive the Holy Ghost by a definite act of faith for his consecration, as he received Christ by faith for his justification, and may he not be sure that he is in a safe and scriptural way of acting?   We know of no plainer form of stating the matter than to speak of it as a simple acceptance by faith, the faith which is

An affirmation and an act,
Which bids eternal truth be present fact.

It is a fact that Christ has made atonement for sin ; in conversion faith appropriates this fact in order to our justification. It is a fact that the Holy Ghost has been given ; in consecration faith appropriates this fact for our sanctification. One who writes upon this subject with a scholarship evidently illuminated by a deep spiritual tuition, says : "If a reference to personal experience may be permitted, I may indeed here 'set my seal.' Never shall I forget the gain to conscious faith and peace which came to my own soul, not long after a first decisive and appropriating view of the crucified Lord as the sinner's sacrifice of peace, from a more intelligent and conscious hold upon the living and most gracious personality of the Spirit through whose mercy the soul had got that blessed view. It was a new development of insight into the love of God. *It was a new contact as it were with the inner and eternal movements of redeeming goodness and power, a new discovery in divine resources.*"[1]

Well is our doctrine described in these italicised words : "*A contact with the inner movements of Divine power.*" The energy of the Spirit appropriated, even as with uplifted finger the electric car touches the current which is moving just above it in the wire and is borne irresistibly on by it.— Thus does the power which is eternally for us become a power within us ; the law of Sinai, with

---

[1] "*Veni Creator Spiritus,*" by Principal H. C. G. Moule, p. 13.

its tables of stone, is replaced by "the law of the Spirit of life" in the fleshly tables of the heart; the outward commandment is exchanged for an inward decalogue; hard duty by holy delight, that henceforth the Christian life may be "all in Christ, by the Holy Spirit, for the glory of God."

VI

THE COMMUNION OF THE SPIRIT

"In his intimate union with his Son, the Holy Spirit is the unique organ by which God wills to communicate to man his own life, the supernatural life, the divine life—that is to say, his holiness, his power, his love, his felicity. To this end the Son works outwardly, the Holy Spirit inwardly."—*Pastor G. F. Tophel.*

VI

THE COMMUNION OF THE SPIRIT

THE familiar benediction which invokes upon us
the "communion of the Holy Ghost" has probably a deeper meaning in it than has generally been
recognized. The word "communion"—κοινωνία—
signifies the having in common. It is used of the
fellowship of believers one with another, and also
of their mutual fellowship with God. The Holy
Spirit dwelling in us is the agent through whom
this community of life and love is effected and
maintained. "And truly our fellowship," says John,
"is with the Father and with his Son Jesus Christ"
(1 John 1 : 3). But this having in common with
the first two persons of the Godhead were only possible through the communion of the Holy Ghost,
the third person. In his promise of the Comforter,
Jesus said : "He shall take of mine and show it
unto you." As the Son while on earth communicated to men the spiritual riches of the invisible
Father, so the Spirit now communicates to us the
hidden things of the invisible Son ; and if we were
required to describe in a word the present office-
work of the Holy Ghost, we should say that it is to
make true *in* us that which is already true *for* us in

99

our glorified Lord. All light and life and warmth are stored up for us in the sun; but these can only reach us through the atmosphere which stands between us and that sun as the medium of communication; even so in Christ are "hidden all the treasures of wisdom and knowledge," and by the Holy Spirit these are made over to us. It will be our endeavor in this chapter to count up our hid treasures in Christ, and to consider the Spirit in his various offices of communication.

1. *The Spirit of Life: Our Regeneration.* Not until our Lord took his place at God's right hand did he assume his full prerogative as life-giver to us. He was here in the flesh for our death; he took on him our nature that he might in himself crucify our Adam-life and put it away. But when he rose from the dead and sat down on his Father's throne, he became the life-giver to all his mystical body, which is the church. To talk of being saved by the earthly life of Jesus is to know Christ only "after the flesh." True, the apostle says that "being reconciled" by Christ's death, "much more being reconciled we shall be saved by his life." But he here refers plainly to his glorified life. And Jesus, looking forward to the time when he should have risen from the dead, says: "Because I live, ye shall live also." Christ on the throne is really the heart of the church, and every regeneration is a pulse-beat of that heart in souls begotten from above

through the Holy Spirit. The new birth therefore is not a change of nature as it is sometimes defined; it is rather the communication of the Divine nature, and the Holy Spirit is now the Mediator through whom this life is transmitted. If we take our Lord's words to Nicodemus: "Except a man be born again he cannot see the kingdom of God," and press the "again" ἄνωθεν back to its deepest significance, it becomes very instructive. "Born *from above*," say some. And very true to fact is this saying. Regeneration is not our natural life carried up to its highest point of attainment, but the Divine life brought down to its lowest point of condescension, even to the heart of fallen man. John, in speaking of Jesus as the life-giver, calls him "*he that cometh from above*" (3 : 31); and Jesus, in speaking to the degenerate sons of Abraham, says: "Ye are *from beneath*, I am *from above*" (John 8 : 23). It has been the constant dream and delusion of men that they could rise to heaven by the development and improvement of their natural life. Jesus by one stroke of revelation destroys this hope, telling his hearer that unless he has been begotten of God who is above as truly as he has been begotten of his father on earth, he cannot see the kingdom of God.

Others make these words of our Lord signify "born *from the beginning*." There must be a resumption of life *de novo*, a return to the original source and fountain of being. To find this it is not enough that we go back to the creation-beginning revealed in Genesis; we must return to the pre-creation-beginning revealed in John, the book of re-genesis. In the opening of Genesis we find Adam, created holy, now fallen through temptation, his face averted from God and leading the whole human race after him into sin and death. In the opening of the Gospel of John we find the Son of God in holy fellowship with the Father. "In the beginning was the Word, and the Word was toward God, πρὸς τὸν θεόν—not merely proceeding from God, but tending toward God by eternal communion. Conversion restores man to this lost attitude: "Ye turned to God, πρὸς τὸν θεόν, from idols to serve the living and true God" (1 Thess. 1 : 9). Regeneration restores man to his forfeited life, the unfallen life of the Son of God, the life which has never wavered from steadfast fellowship with the Father. "I give unto them eternal life," says Jesus. Is eternal life without end? Yes; and just as truly without beginning. It is uncreated being in distinction from all-created being; it is the I-am life of God in contrast to the I-become life of all human souls. By spiritual birth we acquire a divine heredity as truly as by natural birth we acquire a human heredity.

In the condensed antithesis with which our Lord concludes his demand for the new birth, we have both the philosophy and the justification of his doctrine : "That which is born of the flesh is flesh, and that which is born of the Spirit is spirit. Marvel not that I say unto you, Ye must be born anew" (John 3 : 7, R. V.). By no process of evolution, however prolonged, can the natural man be developed into the spiritual man ; by no process of degeneration can the spiritual man deteriorate into the natural man. These two are from a totally different stock and origin ; the one is from beneath, the other is from above. There is but one way through which the relation of sonship can be established, and that is by begetting. That God has created all men does not constitute them his sons in the evangelical sense of that word. The sonship on which the New Testament dwells so constantly is based absolutely and solely on the experience of the new birth, while the doctrine of universal sonship rests either upon a daring denial or a daring assumption—the denial of the universal fall of man through sin, or the assumption of the universal regeneration of man through the Spirit. In either case the teaching belongs to "another gospel," the recompense of whose preaching is not a beatitude but an anathema.[1]

The contrast between the two lives and the way

---

[1] Milton probably gives the true genesis of this doctrine in these words, which he puts into the mouth of Satan :

> "The son of God I also am or was;
> And if I was, I am ; relation stands;
> All men are sons of God."

in which the partnership—the κοινωνία—with the new is effected, is told in that deep saying of Peter: "Whereby he hath granted us his precious and exceeding great promises; that through these ye may become partakers—κοινωνοί—of the divine nature, having escaped from the corruption which is in the world by lust" (2 Pet. 1 : 4, R. V.). Here are the two streams of life contrasted:

1   The corruption in the world through lust.

2. The Divine nature which is in the world through the incarnation.

Here is the Adam-life into which we are brought by natural birth; and over against it the Christ-life into which we are brought by spiritual birth. From the one we escape, of the other we partake. The source and issue of the one are briefly summarized: "Lust when it hath conceived bringeth forth sin, and sin when it is finished bringeth forth death." The Jordan is a fitting symbol of our natural life, rising in a lofty elevation and from pure springs, but plunging steadily down till it pours itself into that Dead Sea from which there is no outlet. To be taken out of this stream and to be brought into the life which flows from the heart of God is man's only hope of salvation. And the method of effecting this transition is plainly stated, "through these," or by means of the precious and exceeding great promises. As in grafting, the old and degenerate stock must first be cut off and then the new inserted, so in regeneration we are separated from the flesh and incorporated by the Spirit.   And what the scion is in grafting, the word or promise of God is in regeneration.   It is the medium through which the Holy Spirit is conveyed, the germ cell in which the Divine life is enfolded.   Hence the emphasis which is put in Scripture upon the appropriation of divine truth. We are told that "of his own will begat he us *with the word of truth*" (James 1 : 18).   "Having been begotten again, not of corruptible seed but of incorruptible, *through the word of God*, which liveth and abideth" (1 Peter 1 : 23, R. V.).

Very deep and significant, therefore, is the saying of Jesus in respect to the regenerating power of his words, in the sixth chapter of the Gospel of John. He emphasizes the contrariety between the two natures, the human and the divine, saying : " It is the Spirit that quickeneth, the flesh profiteth nothing."   And then he adds : "The words which I have spoken unto you are spirit and life."   As God in creation breathed into man the breath of life and he became a living soul, so the Lord Jesus by the word of his mouth, which is the breath of life, recreates man and makes him alive unto God.   And not life only, but likeness as well, is thus imparted. " So God created man in his own image ; in the image of God created he him," is the simple story of the origin of an innocent race.   Then follows the temptation and the fall, and then the story of the descent of a ruined humanity : " And Adam begot a son in his own likeness, after his image."

And yet how wide the gulf between these two origins.   The notion is persistent and incurable in the human heart, that whatever variation there may have been from the original type, education and training can reshape the likeness of Adam to the likeness of God.   " As the twig is bent the tree is inclined," says the popular proverb.   True; but though a crooked sapling may be developed into the upright oak, no bending or manipulation can ever so change the species of the tree as to enable men to gather grapes of thorns or figs of thistles.   Here again the dualism of Jesus Christ's teaching is distinctly recognized.   " A good tree cannot bring forth evil fruit, neither can a corrupt tree bring forth good fruit."   And what is the remedy for a corrupt tree? The cutting off of the old and the bringing in of a new scion and stock.   The life of God can alone beget the likeness of God; the divine type is wrapped up in the same germ which holds the Divine nature.   Therefore in regeneration we are said to have " put on the new man who is renewed in knowledge *after the image of him that created him*" (Col. 3 : 10), and " which *after God* hath been created in   .   .   .   true holiness" (Eph. 4 : 24).

In a word, the lost image of God is not restamped upon us, but renewed within us.   Christ our life was " begotten of the Holy Ghost," and he became

the fount and origin of life henceforth for all
his church. This communication of the divine
life from Christ to the soul through the Holy Spirit
is a hidden transaction, but so great in its significance and issues that one has well called it "the
greatest of all miracles." As in the origin of our
natural life we are made in secret and curiously
wrought, much more in our spiritual. But the issue
has to do with the farthest eternity. "As when the
Lord was born the world still went on its old way,
little conscious that one had come who should one
day change and rule all things, so when the new
man is framed within, the old life for a while goes
on much as before; the daily calling, and the earthly
cares, and too often old lusts and habits also, still en-
gross us; a worldly eye sees little new, while yet
the life which shall live forever has been quickened
within and a new man been formed who shall inherit all." [1]

2. *The Spirit of Holiness: Our Sanctification.*
"According to the Spirit of holiness" Christ "was
declared to be the Son of God in power by the resurrection from the dead" (Rom. 1 : 4). How striking the antithesis between our Lord's two natures,
as revealed in this passage, Son of David as to the
flesh, Son of God as to the Spirit. And "as he is so
are we in this world." We who are regenerate have
two natures, the one derived from Adam, the other

---

[1] Andrew Jukes, "The New Man," p. 53.

derived from Christ, and our sanctification consists in the double process of mortification and vivification, the deadening and subduing of the old and the quickening and developing of the new. In other words, what was wrought in Christ who was " put to death in the flesh but quickened in the spirit " is rewrought in us through the constant operation of the Holy Ghost, and thus the cross and the resurrection extend their sway over the entire life of the Christian. Consider these two experiences.

Mortification is not asceticism. It is not a self-inflicted compunction, but a Christ-inflicted crucifixion. Our Lord was done with the cross when on Calvary he cried : " It is finished." But where he ended each disciple must begin : " If any man will come after me let him deny himself and take up his cross and follow me. For whosoever will save his life shall lose it, and whosoever will lose his life for my sake shall find it " (Matt. 16 : 24, 25). These words, so constantly repeated in one form or another by our Lord, make it clear that the death-principle must be realized within us in order that the life-principle may have final and triumphant sway. It is to this truth which every disciple is solemnly committed in his baptism : " Know ye not that so many of us as were baptized into Christ were baptized into his death ? Therefore we were buried with him by baptism into death, that **like as** Christ was raised up from the dead by the glory of the Father, even so we also should walk in newness of life" (Rom. 6 : 3, 4). Baptism is the monogram of the Christian; by it every believer is sealed and certified as a participant in the death and life of Christ; and the Holy Spirit has been given to be the Executor of the contract thus made at the symbolic grave of Christ.

In considering the great fact of the believer's death in Christ to sin and the law, we must not confound what the Scriptures clearly distinguish. There are three deaths in which we have part:

1. *Death in sin, our natural condition.*
2. *Death for sin, our judicial condition.*
3. *Death to sin our sanctified condition.*

1. *Death in sin.* "And you . . . who were dead in trespasses and sins," "And you being dead in your sins" (Eph. 2 : 1 ; Col. 2 : 13). This is the condition in which we are by nature, as participants in the fall and ruin into which the transgression of our first parents has plunged the race. It is a condition in which we are under moral insensibility to the claims of God's holiness and love; and under the sentence of eternal punishment from the law which we have broken. In this state of death in sin Christ found the whole world when he came to be our Saviour.

2. *Death for sin.* "Wherefore, my brethren, ye also are become dead to the law by the body of Christ" (Rom. 7 : 4). This is the condition into

which Christ brought us by his sacrifice upon the cross. He endured the sentence of a violated law on our behalf, and therefore we are counted as having endured it in him. What he did for us is reckoned as having been done by us: "Because we thus judge, that one died for all, therefore all died" (2 Cor. 5 : 14, R. V.). Being one with Christ through faith, we are identified with him on the cross: "I have been crucified with Christ" (Gal. 2 : 20, R. V.). This condition of death for sin having been effected for us by our Saviour, we are held legally or judicially free from the penalty of a violated law, if by our personal faith we will consent to the transaction.

3. *Death to sin.* "Even so reckon ye also yourselves to be dead unto sin, but alive unto God in Christ Jesus" (Rom. 6 : 11, R. V.). This is the condition of making true in ourselves what is already true for us in Christ, of rendering practical what is now judicial; in other words, of being dead to the power of sin in ourselves, as we are already dead to the penalty of sin through Jesus Christ. As it is written in the Epistle to the Colossians: "For ye died," judicially in Christ, "mortify"—make dead practically—"therefore your members which are upon the earth" (Col. 3 : 2, 5, R. V.). It is this condition which the Holy Spirit is constantly effecting in us if we will have it so. "If ye through the Spirit do mortify the deeds of the body

ye shall live " (Rom. 8 : 13).   This is not self
deadening, as the Revised Version seems to suggest
by its decapitalizing of the word " Spirit."   Self is
not powerful enough to conquer self, the human
spirit to get the victory over the human flesh.
That were like a drowning man with his right hand
laying hold on his left hand, only that both may
sink beneath the waves.   " Old Adam is too strong
for young Melancthon," said the Reformer.   It is
the Spirit of God overcoming our fleshly nature by
his indwelling life, on whom is our sole dependence.
Our principal care therefore must be to " walk in
the Spirit " and " be filled with the Spirit," and all
the rest will come spontaneously and inevitably.
As the ascending sap in the tree crowds off the
dead leaves which in spite of storm and frost cling
to the branches all winter long, so does the Holy
Ghost within us, when allowed full sway, subdue
and expel the remnants of our sinful nature.

One cannot fail to see that asceticism is an absolute inversion of the Divine order, since it seeks
life through death instead of finding death through
life.   No degree of mortification can ever bring us
to sanctification.   We are to " put off the old man
with his deeds."   But how ?   By " putting on the
new man who is renewed in knowledge after the
image of him that created him."   " For the law of
the Spirit of life in Christ Jesus hath made me
free from the law of sin and death " (Rom. 8 : 2),

writes Paul. It is a pointed statement of the case which one makes in describing the transition from the old to the new in his own experience, from the former life of perpetual defeat to the present life of victory through Christ. "Once it was a constant breaking off, now it is a daily bringing in," he says. That is, the former striving was directed to being rid of the inveterate habits and evil tendencies of the old nature—its selfishness, its pride, its lust, and its vanity. Now the effort is to bring in the Spirit, to drink in his divine presence, to breathe, as a holy atmosphere, his supernatural life. The indwelling of the Spirit can alone effect the exclusion of sin. This will appear if we consider what has been called "the expulsive power of a new affection." "Love not the world, neither the things that are in the world," says the Scripture. But all experience proves that loving not is only possible through loving, the worldly affection being overcome by the heavenly.

And we find this method clearly exhibited in the word. "The love of the Spirit" (Rom. 15 : 30) is given us for overcoming the world. The divine life is the source of the divine love. Therefore "the love of God is shed abroad in our hearts by the Holy Ghost which is given unto us." Because we are by nature so wholly without heavenly affection, God, through the indwelling Spirit, gives us his own love with which to love himself. Herein is the highest credential of discipleship : "By this shall all men know that ye are my disciples, if ye have love one to another" (John 13 : 35). As Christ manifested to the world the love of the Father, so are we to manifest the love of Christ—a manifestation, however, which is only possible because of our possessorship of a common life. As one has truly said concerning our Saviour's command to his disciples to love one another : "It is a command which would be utterly idle and futile were it not that he, the ever-loving One, is willing to put his own love within me. The command is really no more than to be a branch of the true vine. I am to cease from my own living and loving, and yield myself to the expression of Christ's love."

And what is true of the love of Christ is true of the likeness of Christ. How is the likeness acquired? Through contemplation and imitation? So some have taught. And it is true, if only the indwelling Spirit is behind all, beneath all, and effectually operative in all. As it is written : "But we all with unveiled face, reflecting as a mirror the glory of the Lord, are transformed into the same image from glory to glory, even as from the Lord, the Spirit" (2 Cor. 3 : 18, R. V.). It is only the Spirit of the Lord dwelling within us that can fashion us to the image of the Lord set before us. Who is sufficient by external imitation of Christ to become conformed to the likeness of Christ? Imagine one without genius and devoid of the artist's training sitting down before Raphael's famous picture of the Transfiguration and attempting to reproduce it. How crude and mechanical and lifeless his work would be! But if such a thing were possible that the spirit of Raphael should enter into the man and obtain the mastery of his mind and eye and hand, it would be entirely possible that he should paint this masterpiece; for it would simply be Raphael reproducing Raphael. And this in a mystery is what is true of the disciple filled with the Holy Ghost. Christ, who is "the image of the invisible God," is set before him as his divine pattern, and Christ by the Spirit dwells within him as a divine life, and Christ is able to image forth Christ from the interior life to the outward example.

Of course likeness to Christ is but another name for holiness, and when, at the resurrection, we awake satisfied with his likeness (Ps. 17 : 15), we shall be perfected in holiness. This is simply saying that sanctification is progressive and not, like conversion, instantaneous. And yet we must admit the force of what a devout and thoughtful writer says as to the danger of regarding it as *only* a gradual growth. If a Christian looks upon himself as "a tree planted by the rivers of water that bringeth forth his fruit in his season," he judges rightly. But to conclude therefore that his growth will be as irresistible as that of the tree, coming as a matter of course simply because he has by regeneration been planted in Christ, is a grave mistake. The disciple is required to be consciously and intelligently active in his own growth, as a tree is not, "to give all diligence to make his calling and election sure." And when we say "active" we do not mean self-active merely, for "which of you by being anxious can add one cubit unto his stature?" asks Jesus (Matt. 6: 27, R. V.). But we must surrender ourselves to the divine action by living in the Spirit and praying in the Spirit and walking in the Spirit, all of which conditions are as essential to our development in holiness, as the rain and the sunshine are to the growth of the oak. It is possible that through a neglect and grieving of the Spirit a Christian may be of smaller stature in his age than he was in his spiritual infancy, his progress being a retrogression rather than an advance. Therefore in saying that sanctification is progressive let us beware of concluding that it is inevitable.

Moreover, as candid inquirers, we must ask what of truth and of error there may be in the doctrine of "instantaneous sanctification," which many devout persons teach and profess to have proved. If the conception is that of a state of sinless perfection into which the believer has been suddenly lifted and of deliverance from a sinful nature which has been suddenly eradicated, we must consider this doctrine as dangerously untrue. But we do consider it possible that one may experience a great crisis in his spiritual life, in which there is such a total self-surrender to God and such an in-filling of the Holy Spirit, that he is freed from the bondage of sinful appetites and habits, and enabled to have constant victory over self, instead of suffer-ing constant defeat. In saying this, what more do we affirm than is taught in that scripture : " Walk in the Spirit and ye shall not fulfill the lust of the flesh" (Gal. 5 : 16).

Divine truth as revealed in Scripture seems often to lie between two extremes. It is emphatically so in regard to this question. What a paradox it is that side by side in the Epistle of John we should have the strongest affirmation of the Christian's sinful-ness : " If we say that we have no sin we deceive ourselves, and the truth is not in us "; and the strong-est affirmation of his sinlessness : " Whosoever is born of God doth not commit sin, for his seed remain-eth in him, and he cannot sin because he is born of God" (1 John 1 : 8 ; 3 : 9). Now heresy means a dividing or choosing, and almost all of the gravest errors have arisen from adopting some extreme statement of Scripture to the rejection of the other extreme. If we regard the doctrine of sinless per-fection as a heresy, we regard contentment with sin-ful imperfection as a greater heresy. And we gravely fear that many Christians make the apos-

tle's words, "If we say we have no sin we deceive
ourselves," the unconscious justification for a low
standard of Christian living.   It were almost better
for one to overstate the possibilities of sanctification in his eager grasp after holiness, than to under-
state them in his complacent satisfaction with a
traditional unholiness.   Certainly it is not an edi-
fying spectacle to see a Christian worldling throw-
ing stones at a Christian perfectionist.

What then would be a true statement of the
doctrine which we are considering, one which would
embrace both extremes of statement as they appear
in the Epistle of John ?   *Sinful in self, sinless in
Christ*—is our answer : "In him is no sin ; whosoever abideth in him sinneth not" (1 John 3 : 5, 6).
If through the communication of the Holy Spirit
the life of Christ is constantly imparted to us, that
life will prevail within us.   That life is absolutely
sinless, as incapable of defilement as the sunbeam
which has its fount and origin in the sun.   In proportion to the closeness of our abiding in him will
be the completeness of our deliverance from sinning.   And we doubt not that there are Christians
who have yielded themselves to God in such absolute surrender, and who through the upholding
power of the Spirit have been so kept in that condition of surrender, that sin has not had dominion
over them.   If in them the war between the flesh
and the spirit has not been forever ended, there has

been present victory in which troublesome sins have ceased from their assaults, and "the peace of God" has ruled in the heart.

But sinning is one thing and a sinful nature is another; and we see no evidence in Scripture that the latter is ever eradicated completely while we are in the body. If we could see ourselves with God's eye, we should doubtless discover sinfulness lying beneath our most joyful moments of unsinning con- duct, and the stain of our old and fallen nature so discoloring our whitest actions as to convince us that we are not yet faultless in his presence. Only let us gladly emphasize this fact, that as we inherit from Adam a nature incapable of sinlessness, we inherit from Christ a nature incapable of sinfulness. Therefore, it is written: "Whosoever is born of God cannot sin, for his seed remaineth in him." It is not the nature of the new nature to sin; it is not the law of "the law of the Spirit of life" to transgress. For the new-born man to do evil is to transgress the law of his nature as before it was to obey it. In a word, before our regeneration we lived in sin and loved it; since our regeneration we may lapse into sin but we loathe it.

3. *The Spirit of Glory: Our Transfiguration.* "The Spirit of glory and of God resteth upon you," writes Peter (1 Peter 4 : 14). Let us recall this apostle's habit of dividing the stages of redemption into these two, "the sufferings of Christ and the

glory that should follow," in which he seems to conceive of our Lord's mystical body, the church, as passing through and reproducing the twofold experience of its Head, in humiliation and in subsequent exaltation. Even in the time of her humiliation she has the Spirit of glory abiding on her, as the cloud of glory rested down upon the tabernacle in the wilderness during all the pilgrimage of the children of Israel. And is not Peter's saying the same as Paul's, in his picture of the suffering creation : " But ourselves also, which have the first fruits of the Spirit, even we ourselves groan within ourselves, waiting for the adoption, to wit, the redemption of our body " (Rom. 8 : 23). Not yet have we reached the consummation of our hope, at the "appearing of the glory of our great God and Saviour Jesus Christ " (Titus 2 : 13, R. V.) ; but the Spirit, through whose inworking power this great change is to be wrought, already dwells in us, giving us by his present quickening the pledge and earnest of our final glory. And so we read in another Scripture : " But if the Spirit of him that raised up Jesus from the dead dwell in you, he that raised up Christ from the dead shall also quicken your mortal bodies by his Spirit that dwelleth in you" (Rom. 8 : 11). It is not our dead bodies which are here spoken of as the objects of the Spirit's quickening, but our mortal bodies—bodies liable to death and doomed to death if the Lord tarry, but not yet having experienced death. Hence the quickening referred to has to do rather with the vivifying of the living saints than the resurrection of the dead saints.

Of course the consummation of this vivifying is at the Lord's coming, when those who have died shall be raised, and those who are alive shall be transfigured ; but because of the Spirit of life dwelling in us, who shall say that the process has not even now begun ? To explain : " Behold I shew you a mystery," says Paul ; " we shall not all sleep, but we shall all be changed, in a moment, in the twinkling of an eye, at the last trump " (1 Cor. 15 : 51, 52).   That is, as at Christ's coming the dead saints will be raised, so the living saints will be translated without seeing death.   A change will come to them, so far as we can understand, like that which came to Jesus at his resurrection—the body glorified, all of mortal and earthly belonging to it by nature eliminated in an instant, and the Holy Ghost so completely transforming and immortalizing it that it shall become perfectly fashioned to the likeness of Christ's glorified body.   But having the Spirit dwelling in us we have, even now, the first-fruits of this transformation in the daily renewing of our inward man, in the helping and healing and strengthening which sometimes comes to our bodies through the hidden life of the Holy Ghost.   Sanctification is progressive, waiting to be consummated in the future; so is glorification in some sense progressive, since by the presence of the Spirit we already have the earnest of the glory that is to be. As Edward Irving beautifully states it, condensing his language: "As sickness is sin apparent in the body, the presentiment of death, the forerunner of corruption, and as disease of every kind is mortality begun, so the quickening of our mortal bodies by the inward inspiration of the Spirit is the resurrection forestalled, redemption anticipated, glory begun in our humiliation."

When is sanctification completed? At death, is the answer which we find given in some creeds and manuals of theology. This may be true; but we say it not, because the Scripture saith it not. So far as we can infer from the word of God the date of our sanctification or perfection in holiness is definitely fixed at the appearing of the Lord "a second time without sin unto salvation." Our sanctification, now going on, is glory begun in us; our glorification then ushered in will be glory completed in us. The Spirit of glory now working in us brings forward and already works within us the beginning of the perfect life. Because we have been made "partakers of the Holy Ghost" we have thereby "tasted the powers of the age to come" (Heb. 6 : 4, 5, R. V.), that age of complete deliverance from sin and sickness and death. But at most we have only tasted as yet; we have not drunk fully into the fountain of immortal life. It is at Christ's advent that this blessed consummation is fixed: "To the end he may establish your hearts unblamable in holiness before our God and Father *at the coming of our Lord Jesus with all his saints*" (1 Thess. 3 : 13, R. V.). Not simply blameless but faultless, seems to be the condition here foretold, since it is unblamable in the sphere and element of holiness.

And with this agrees another text in the same epistle: "And the God of peace himself sanctify you wholly; and may your spirit and soul and body be preserved entire without blame *at the coming of our Lord Jesus Christ*" (1 Thess. 5 : 23, R. V.). The time appointed for the consummation of this blameless wholeness is at the Saviour's advent in glory. And how suggestive the order maintained in naming the threefold man: "Your spirit, soul, and body." Our sanctification moves from within outward. It begins with the spirit, which is the holy of holies; the Spirit of God acting first on the spirit of man in renewing grace, then upon the soul, till at last it reaches the outer court of the body, at the resurrection and translation. When the body is glorified, then only will sanctification be consummated, for then only will the whole man, spirit, soul, and body, have come under the Spirit's perfecting power.

We may see the difference between progressive

sanctification and perfected sanctification, or glorification, by comparing familiar texts.   One already
has been quoted in this chapter :   " We all, beholding as in a glass the glory of the Lord, are changed
into the same image from glory to glory, even
as by the Spirit of the Lord" (2 Cor. 3 : 18). Here
are degrees of progress "from glory to glory,"
and it is a progress in the glorified life—gradual
conformity to the Lord of glory, through successive stages of glory, effected by the Spirit of glory.
The word-painting of the passage inevitably asso-
ciates it in our thought with the great transfiguration experience of our Lord, when by a kind of
rapture he was for a little while taken out of "this
present evil age " (Gal. 1 : 4), and translated into
" the age to come," and made to taste of its powers
as he appeared in glory" (Heb. 6 : 5, R. V.).   So
says the apostle :   " Be not fashioned *according to
this age*, but be ye transformed by the renewing of
your minds " (Rom. 12 : 2, R. V.).   That is, by his
inward transformation the Holy Spirit is to be daily
repeating in us the Lord's glorification, separating
us from the present age of sin and death and as-
similating us to the age to come, with its resurrec-
tioi triumph and its perfected restoration to God,
when we shall be presented "faultless before the
presence of his glory with exceeding joy " (Jude.24).
This is our step-by-step advancement into a predestined inheritance ; and it must for the present be

step by step. "Of his fullness have all we received," but we can appropriate that fullness only "grace by grace" (John 1 : 16). Of his righteousness we have all been made partakers, but we only advance in its possession "from faith to faith" (Rom. 1 : 17). Even in passing through the valley of Baca we can make it a place of springs, going "from strength to strength" as we appear "before God in Zion" (Ps. 84 : 6). Thus our growth in grace is our glory begun; but the progress is like the artist's slow and patient perfecting of his picture. Turn now to another statement: "We know that if he shall be manifested we shall be like him, for we shall see him even as he is" (1 John 3 : 2, R. V.). Whatever difficulty may arise from another translation of this passage, one thought seems to be taught in the entire connection, viz., that the unveiled manifestation of God will bring the full perfection of his saints. Thus Alford sums up the meaning of the passage. As the believer, having by a knowledge of God been regenerated, "becomes more and more like God, having his seed in him, so the full and perfect accomplishment of this knowledge in the actual fruition of God himself must of necessity bring with it entire likeness to God." In a word, it seems to us that the sanctification taking place at the manifestation of our incarnate Lord will be as the instantaneous photograph compared with the Spirit's slow and patient limning of the image of Christ in our present state. "In a moment, in the twinkling of an eye," "we shall be changed" (1 Cor. 15 : 52). Then the glorified body and the glorified spirit, long divorced by sin, will be remarried. So long as this twain are separated by death, or are at war in our present earthy life, our perfection in holiness were impossible.

It is because the resurrection and translation of the saints are instantaneous that we affirm sanctification to be instantaneous at the coming of the Lord. The Scripture is always harmonious with itself, however widely separated the writers of its books by time or distance. David struck the same joyful note with John, though the learned may insist that he did not know of the resurrection. "As for me, I shall behold thy face in righteousness"—the seeing him as he is and being made fit to see him. "I shall be satisfied when I awake in thy likeness"—the conformity to the Divine image at the instant sound of the resurrection trump. (Ps. 17 : 15.) Perhaps we may conjecture wherein will consist the perfection of the resurrection state. We may find it in that one saying : "It is raised a spiritual body" (1 Cor. 15 : 44). *Now*, how often the body dominates the spirit, making it do what it would not ; but *then*, the spirit will dominate the body, making it do as it will. In a house divided against itself there can be neither perfection nor peace. Such is the condition in our present state of humiliation.   And not the body alone, but the immaterial within us may be at war with the divine. What does the Apostle Jude mean in his description of certain who separated themselves, saying that they are "sensual, having not the Spirit" (Jude 19).   The soul, the middle factor in the man, if we may say so, instead of being in alliance with our higher nature, the spirit, takes sides with the lower, the flesh, so that instead of being spiritual we become "earthly, sensual, devilish" (James 3 : 15).   The whole man must be presented blameless at the coming of the Lord before we can enter upon a state of blessed perfection.   Our spirit must not only rule our soul and our body, but both these must be subject to the Holy Spirit of God. Dimly and imperfectly do we thus image to ourselves the perfection of our "spiritual body."   Now the body bears the spirit, a slow chariot, whose wheels are often disabled, and whose swiftest motion is but labored and tardy.   Then the spirit will bear the body, carrying it as on wings of thought whithersoever it will.   The Holy Ghost, by his divine inworking will, has completed in us the Divine likeness, and perfected over us the Divine dominion. The human body will now be in sovereign subjection to the human spirit, and the human spirit to the divine Spirit, and God will be all and in all.

VII

THE ADMINISTRATION OF THE SPIRIT

" The Holy Ghost from the day of Pentecost has occupied an entirely new position. The whole administration of the affairs of the Church of Christ has since that day devolved upon him. . . That day was the installation of the Holy Spirit as the Administrator of the Church in all things, which office he is to exercise according to circumstances at his discretion. It is as vested with such authority that he gives his name to this dispensation. . . There is but one other great event to which the Scripture directs us to look, and that is the second coming of the Lord. Till then we live in the Pentecostal age and under the rule of the Holy Ghost."—*James Elder Cumming, D. D.*

VII

THE ADMINISTRATION OF THE SPIRIT

THE Holy Spirit, as coming down to fill the place of the ascended Redeemer, has rightly been called "The Vicar of Jesus Christ." To him the entire administration of the church has been committed until the Lord shall return in glory. His oversight extends to the slightest detail in the ordering of God's house, holding all in subjection to the will of the Head, and directing all in harmony with the divine plan. How clearly this comes out in that passage in the twelfth chapter of First Corinthians. As in striking a series of concentric circles there is always one fixed center holding each circumference in defined relation to itself, so here we see all the "diversities of administrations" determined by the one Administrator, the Holy Ghost. "Varieties of gifts, but *the same Spirit*"; "diversities of working, but *the same God*"; different words "according to *the same Spirit*"; "gifts of faith *in the same Spirit*"; "gifts of healing *in the one Spirit*"; miracles, prophecies, tongues, interpretations, "but all these worketh the *one and the same Spirit*, dividing to each one severally as he will." Whether the authority of this one ruling sovereign Holy Ghost be recognized or ignored determines whether the church shall be an anarchy or a unity, a synagogue of lawless ones or the temple of the living God.

Would one desire to find the clue to the great apostasy whose dark eclipse now covers two-thirds of nominal Christendom, here it is—the rule and authority of the Holy Spirit ignored in the church; the servants of the house assuming mastery and encroaching more and more on the prerogatives of the Head, till at last one man sets himself up as the administrator of the church, and daringly usurps the name of "The Vicar of Christ." When the Spirit of the Lord, speaking by Paul, would picture the mystery of lawlessness and the culmination of apostasy, he gives us a description which none should misunderstand: "So that he, as God, sitteth in the temple of God, shewing himself that he is God" (2 Thess. 2 : 4). What is the temple of God? The church without a question : "Know ye not that ye are the temple of God, and that the Spirit of God dwelleth in you?" (1 Cor. 3 : 16). Whose prerogative is it to sit there? The Holy Ghost's, its ruler and administrator, and his alone.

When Christ, our Paraclete with the Father, entered upon his ministry on high, we are told more than a score of times that he "sat down at the right hand of God." Henceforth heaven is his official seat, until he returns in power and great glory.

When he sent down another Paraclete to abide with us for the age, he took his seat in the church, the temple of God, there to rule and to administer till the Lord returns. There is but one "Holy See" upon earth: that is, the seat of the Holy One in the church, which only the Spirit of God can occupy without the most daring blasphemy. It becomes all true believers to look well to that picture of one "sitting in the temple of God," and to read the lesson which it teaches. We may have no temptation toward the papacy, which thrusts a man into the seat of the Holy Ghost,[1] or toward clerisy which obtrudes an order of ecclesiastics—archbishops, cardinals, and archdeacons into that sacred place; but let us remember that a democracy may be guilty of the same sin as a hierarchy, in settling solemn issues by a "show of hands," instead of prayerfully waiting for the guidance of the Holy Spirit, in substituting the voice of a

---

[1] Of course Catholic writers claim that the pope is the "Vicar of Christ" only as being the mouth-piece of the Holy Ghost. But the Spirit has been given to the church as a whole, that is to the body of regenerated believers, and to every member of that body according to his measure. The sin of sacerdotalism is, that it arrogates for a usurping few that which belongs to every member of Christ's mystical body. It is a suggestive fact that the name κλῆρος, which Peter gives to the church as the "flock of God," when warning the elders against being *lords over God's heritage*, now appears in ecclesiastical usage as the *clergy*, with its orders of pontiff and prelates and lord bishops, whose appointed function it is to exercise lordship over Christ's flock.

majority for the voice of the Spirit. Of course, in speaking thus we concede that the Holy Spirit makes known his will in the voice of believers, as also in the voice of Scripture. Only there must be such prayerful sanctifying of the one and such prayerful search of the other, that in reaching decisions in the church there may be the same declaration as in the first Christian council: "It seemed good to the Holy Ghost and to us" (Acts 15 : 28).

In some very profound teaching in 2 Cor. 3 we seem to have a hint as to how we hear the voice of the Lord in guiding the affairs of the church. There the administration (διακονία) of the Spirit is distinctly spoken of in contrast with the administration of the law. Its deliverances are written "not with ink, not in tables of stone, but in the tables that are the hearts of flesh, with the Spirit of the living God" (R. V.). There must be a sensitive heart wherein this handwriting may be inscribed; an unhindering will through which he may act. "Where the Spirit of the Lord is, there is liberty," it is written in the same passage; liberty for God to speak and act as he will through us, which begets loyalty; not liberty for us to act as we will, which begets lawlessness.

To us there is something exceedingly suggestive in the teaching of the Lord's post-ascension gospel, the Revelation, on this point. The epistles to the seven churches we hold, with many of the best commentators, to be a prophetic setting forth of the successive stages of the church's history—its declines and its recoveries, its failures and its repentances, from ascension to advent. And because the bride of Christ is perpetually betrayed into listening to false teachers and surrendering to the guidance of evil counsellors, the Lord is constantly admonishing her to heed the voice of her true Teacher and Guide, the Holy Ghost. How forcibly this admonition is introduced into the great Apocalyptic drama! As in the opening of the successive seals, representing the judgments of God upon apostate Christendom, the cry is repeated, "Come"! "Come"! "Come"! "Come"! (Rev. 6)—as though the church under chastisement would repeatedly relearn the advent prayer which her Lord put into her mouth in the beginning: "Even so, come, Lord Jesus," so at each stage of the church's backsliding a voice is heard from heaven saying: "He that hath an ear, let him hear what the Spirit saith unto the churches." It is the admonition "of him that hath the seven spirits of God," seven times addressed to his church throughout her earthly history, calling her to return from her false guides and misleading teachers, and to listen to the voice of her true Counsellor.

From this general statement of the administration of the Holy Spirit let us now descend to the particular acts and offices in which this authority is exercised.

1. *The Holy Spirit in the ministry and government of the church.* In speaking to the elders of Ephesus Paul says: "Take heed unto yourselves, and to all the flock in the which the Holy Ghost hath made you bishops, to feed the church of God" (Acts 20 : 28, R. V.). Clearly in the beginning bishops or pastors were given by the Spirit of God, not by the suffrages of the people. The office and its incumbent were alike by direct divine appointment. We find this distinctly set forth in the Epistle to the Ephesians : "When he ascended on high, he led captivity captive, and gave gifts unto men. . . And he gave some to be apostles ; and some, prophets ; and some, evangelists ; and some, pastors and teachers ; for the perfecting of the saints, unto the work of ministering, unto the building up of the body of Christ " (Eph. 4 : 8–12, R. V.). The ascent of the Lord and the descent of the Spirit are here exhibited in their necessary relation. In the one event Christ took his seat in heaven as " Head over all things to his church " ; in the other the Holy Ghost came down to begin the work of "building up the body of Christ." Of course it is the Head who directs the construction of the body, as being "fitly framed together it groweth into a holy temple in the Lord"; and it is the Holy Ghost who superintends this construction since "we are

builded together for an habitation of God in the Spirit." Therefore all the offices through which this work is to be carried on were appointed by Christ and instituted through the Spirit whom he sent down. Suppose now that men invent offices which are not named in the inspired list, and set up in the church an order of popes and cardinals, arch-bishops and archdeacons? Is it not a presumption, the worst fruit of which is not alone that it introduces confusion into the body of Christ, but that it begets insubordination to the rule of the Holy Ghost? But suppose, on the other hand, that we sacredly main-tain those offices of the ministry which have been established for permanent continuance in the church, and yet take it upon us to fill these according to our own preference and will; is this any less an affront to the Spirit?

Doubtless the mistakes of God's servants, as given in Scripture are as truly designed for our instruction and admonition as their obedient exam-ples. We think we do not err in finding such a recorded warning in the opening chapter of the Acts of the Apostles. A vacancy had occurred in the apostolate. Standing up in the upper room, amidst the hundred and twenty, Peter boldly affirmed that this vacancy must be filled, and of the men who had companied with them during the Lord's earthly ministry, "one must be ordained to be a witness with us of his resurrection." But the disciples had hitherto had no voice in choosing apostles. The Lord had done this of his own sovereign will: "Have I not chosen you twelve?" Now he had gone away into heaven, and his Administrator had not yet arrived to enter upon his office-work. Surely if the divine order was to be, that having "ascended on high" he was "to give some apostles," it were better to await the coming of the Paraclete with his gifts. Not only so, but we are persuaded that, with Christ departed and the Holy Spirit not yet come, a valid election of an apostle were impossible. But in spite of this, a nomination was made; prayer was offered in which the Lord was asked to indicate which of the candidates he had chosen; and then a vote having been taken, Matthias was declared elected. Is there any indication that this choice was ever ratified by the Lord? On the contrary, Matthias passes into obscurity from this time, his name never again being mentioned. Some two years subsequent, the Lord calls Saul of Tarsus; he is sealed with his Spirit, and certified by such evident credentials of the Divine appointment that he boldly signs himself "Paul, an apostle, *not of men, neither by man, but by Jesus Christ and God the Father*" (Gal. 1 : 1).

We believe that the apostolic office has passed away, the qualification therefor, that of having been a witness of the Lord's resurrection, being now impossible. But the office of pastor, elder, bishop, or teacher of the flock still remains. And the divine plan is that this office should be filled, just as in the beginning, by the appointment of the Holy Ghost. Nor can we doubt that if there is a prayerful waiting upon him for guidance, and a sanctified submission to his will when it is made known, he will now choose pastors and set them over their appointed flocks just as manifestly as he did in the beginning. Very beautiful is the picture in Revelation of the glorified Lord, moving among the candlesticks. There are "seven golden candlesticks" now, not one only as in the Jewish temple. The Church of God is manifold, not a unit.[1] He who "walketh in the midst of the seven golden candlesticks" "holdeth the seven stars in his right hand." These stars are "the angels of the seven churches" —their ministers or bishops as generally understood. The Lord holds them in his right hand. Does he not require us to ask of him alone for their bestowal? Yes. "Pray ye therefore the Lord of the harvest, that he would send forth laborers into his harvest" (Luke 10 : 2). There is no intimation in Scripture that we are to apply anywhere but to him for the ministry of his church. Does he not give

---

[1] By the candlesticks being seven instead of one, as in the tabernacle, we are taught that whereas in the Jewish dispensation, God's visible church was one, in the Gentile dispensation there are many visible churches; and that Christ himself recognizes them alike.— *Canon Garratt, " Commentary on the Revelation," p. 32.*

such ministry, and he alone? Yes. "When he ascended on high . . . he gave some . . . pastors and teachers." And now, speaking to the church in Ephesus, the elders of which, chosen by the Holy Ghost, Paul had so affectionately exhorted, he is seen in the attitude of Chief-shepherd and Bishop—giving pastors with his own hand; placing them with his own right hand, and warning the church that though they have tried and rejected false apostles, they have nevertheless left their "first love." Significant word! On this love our Lord conditioned the indwelling of the Father and of the Son through the Holy Spirit (John 14 : 23). Losing this the peril becomes imminent that the candlestick may be removed out of its place; and so the warning is solemnly announced: "He that hath an ear, let him hear what the Spirit saith unto the churches." Without the Spirit the candlestick can shed forth no light, and loses its place of testimony.

Dead churches, whose witness has been silenced, whose place has been vacated, even though the lifeless form remains, have we not seen such? And what is the safeguard against them, if not that found in the apostle's warning: "Quench not the Spirit?" The voice of the Lord must be heard in his church, and to the Holy Ghost alone has been committed the prerogative of communicating that voice. Is there any likelihood that that voice will be heard when the king or prime minister of a civil government holds the sole function of appointing the bishops, as in the case of State churches? Is there any certainty of it when an archbishop or bishop puts pastors over flocks by the action of his single will? We may congratulate ourselves that we are neither in a State church nor under an episcopal bishop; but there are methods of ignoring or repressing the voice of the Holy Ghost, which though simpler and far less apparent than those just indicated, are no less violent. The humble and godly membership of the little church may turn to some pastor, after much prayer and waiting on God for the Spirit's guidance, and the signs of the divine choice may be clearly manifest; when some pulpit committee, or some conclave of "leading brethren," vetoes their action on the ground, perchance, that the candidate is not popular and will not draw. Alas! for the little flock so lorded over that the voice of the Holy Ghost cannot be heard.

And majorities are no more to be depended upon than minorities, if there is in both cases a neglect of patient and prolonged waiting upon the Lord to know his will. Of what value is a "show of hands" unless his are stretched out "who holdeth the seven stars in his right hand?" Of what use is a *viva voce* choice, except the living voice of Christ be heard speaking by his Spirit? One may object that we are holding up an ideal which is impossible to be realized. It is a difficult ideal we admit, as

the highest attainments are always difficult , but it
is not an impossible one. It is easier to recite our
prayers from a book than to read them from the
tab.es of a prepared heart, where the finger of the
Spirit has silently written them ; but the more
difficult way is the more acceptable way to him who
seeks for worshipers who "worship in Spirit and in
truth." It is easier to get "the sense of the meeting" in choosing a pastor than to learn "the mind
of the Spirit" by patient tarrying and humble surrender to God ; but the more laborious way will
certainly prove the more profitable way. The failure to take this way is, we are persuaded, the cause
of more decay and spiritual death in the churches
than we have yet imagined. From the watch-
tower where we write we can look out on half a
score of churches on which "Ichabod" has been
evidently written, and the glory of which has long
since departed. They were founded in prayer and
consecration, "to serve the living and true God,
and to wait for his Son from heaven." Why has
their light been extinguished, though the lampstand
which once bore it still remains, adorned and beau-
tified with all that the highest art and architecture
can suggest? Their history is known to him who
walks among the golden candlesticks. What violence
may have been done, by headstrong self-will, to him
who is called "the Spirit of counsel and might"?
What rejection of the truth which he, "the Spirit

of truth," has appointed for the faith of God's church till at last the word has been spoken: "Ye do always resist the Holy Ghost; as your fathers did, so do ye." Is it only Jewish worshipers to whom these words apply? Is it only a Jewish temple of which this sentence is true: "Behold your house is left unto you desolate"? The Spirit will not be entirely withdrawn from the body of Christ indeed, but there is the Church, and there are churches. A man may yet live and breathe when cell after cell has been closed by congestion till at last he only inhales and exhales with a little portion of one lung. Let him that readeth understand.

The Spirit is the breath of God in the body of his church. While that divine body survives and must, multitudes of churches have so shut out the Spirit from rule and authority and supremacy in the midst of them that the ascended Lord can only say to them: "Thou hast a name to live and art dead." In a word, so vital and indispensable is the ministry of the Spirit, that without it nothing else will avail. Some trust in creeds, and some in ordinances; some suppose that the church's security lies in a sound theology, and others locate it in a primitive simplicity of government and worship; but it lies in none of these, desirable as they are. The body may be as to its organs perfect and entire, wanting nothing; but simply because the Spirit has been withdrawn from it, it has passed from a church into a corpse. As one has powerfully stated it : " When the Holy Spirit withdraws, . . . he sometimes allows the forms which he has created to remain. The oil is exhausted, but the lamp is still there; prayer is offered and the Bible read ; church-going is not given up, and to a certain degree the service is enjoyed ; in a word religious habits are preserved, and like the corpses found at Pompeii, which were in a perfect state of preservation and in the very position in which death had surprised them, but which were reduced to ashes by contact with the air, so the blast of trial, of temptation, or of final judgment will destroy these spiritual corpses." [1]

2. *The Holy Spirit in the Worship and Service of the Church.* Is there anything, from highest to lowest, which we are called to do in connection with the worship of God's house, of which the Holy Spirit is not the appointed agent ? Believers are the instruments indeed through which he acts ; but they have no function apart from his inspiration and guidance, any more than the organ-pipe has without the wind, which breathing through it causes it to resound. To make this clear, we may consider the several parts of the service of the church as we are accustomed to participate in it, and observe their relation to the divine Administrator.

---

[1] " The Work of the Holy Spirit in Man," by Pastor G. F. Tophel, p. 66.

(1) Preaching is by general consent an important factor of the work of the ministry, both for the pastor and for the evangelist. In what consists its inspiration and authority? We " have preached the gospel unto you *with the Holy Ghost sent down from heaven*" (1 Peter 1 : 12), is Peter's simple story of the apostolic method. And the words direct our thought to the Spirit not as instrumental but as inspiring. "*In the Holy Ghost*," the words mean literally. The true preacher does not simply use the Spirit ; he is used by the Spirit. He speaks as one moving in the element and atmosphere of the Holy Ghost, and mastered by his divine power.

In this fact the sermon differs immeasurably from the speech, and the preacher from the orator. How distinctly Paul emphasizes this contrast in his letter to the Corinthians (1 Cor. 2 : 4). The sole substance of his preaching he declares to be " Jesus Christ and him crucified," and the sole inspiration of his preaching, the Holy Ghost : "And my speech was not with enticing words of man's wisdom, but in demonstration of the Spirit and power." What did good Philip Henry mean by his resolve "to preach Christ crucified in a crucified style"? More perhaps than he thought or knew. "He shall testify of me," is Jesus' saying concerning the promised Paraclete. The Comforter bears witness to the Crucified. No other theme in the pulpit can be sure of commanding his co-operation. Philosophy, poetry, art, literature, sociology, ethics, and history are attractive subjects to many minds, and they who handle such themes in the pulpit may set them forth with alluring words of human genius; but there is no certainty that the Holy Ghost will accompany their presentation with his divine attestation. The preaching of the Cross, in chastened simplicity of speech, has the demonstration of the Spirit pledged to it, as no secular, or moral, or even formal religious discourse has. And when Paul writes to the Thessalonians: "Our gospel came not unto you in word only, but also *in power and in the Holy Ghost,* and in much assurance" (1 Thess. 1 : 5), we need only to be reminded that "our gospel" meant but one thing to Paul, the setting forth of Jesus Christ crucified in the midst of the people, and we have found the secret of evangelical power. Ought it not therefore to be the supreme question with the preacher, what themes can assuredly command the witness of the Holy Spirit, rather than what topics will enlist the attention of the people? Let us set the popular preacher and the apostolic preacher side by side, and consider whose reward we would choose, universal admiration or "God also bearing witness, both with signs and wonders and with divers miracles, and *gifts of the Holy Ghost,* according to his will" (Heb. 2 : 4) —the sermon greeted with applause and the clapping of hands, or "*the word received with joy of the Holy Ghost*" (1 Thess. 1 : 6)?—admiration of the preacher possessing all who listen to the discourse, or "*the Holy Ghost fell on all them which heard the word*" (Acts 10 : 44)? Language cannot express the vital moment of the question which we are here discussing.   Our generation is rapidly losing its grip upon the supernatural; and as a consequence the pulpit is rapidly dropping to the level of the platform. And this decline is due, we believe, more than anything else, to an ignoring of the Holy Spirit as the supreme inspirer of preaching.   We wish to see a great orator in the pulpit, forgetting that the least expounder of the word, when filled with the Holy Ghost, is greater than he.   We want the gospel, forsooth; but in the strenuous demand that it be set forth according to the "spirit of the age" we ignore the supremacy of the "Spirit of God."   And the method of discourse soon tells upon the matter.   We cannot very long have the truth in the pulpit after we have lost "the Spirit of truth " therefrom.   " When one possesses not the whole of life," says Vinet, " he possesses not the whole of truth."

In all that we have said we do not ignore the human element in preaching, nor undervalue good learning and sanctified mental training, as a furnishing for this high office.   We only emphasize the extreme peril of making that supreme which God has made subordinate.   As it is genius which raises the great painter or poet far above the common man, so it is the Holy Spirit which lifts the preacher far above the man of genius. A gifted artist spoke wisely when one, thinking only of the implements of his profession, asked, "With what do you mix your paints?" "With brains, sir," he replied. The preacher who brought three thousand to believe on a crucified Christ, under a single sermon, antici- pated the question of those who, with an eye upon the mere human accessories of his sermon, might ask after the secret of his power; and he unfolds that secret in a single terse sentence: "With the Holy Ghost sent down from heaven."

(2) Prayer is a most vital element in the worship of God's church. "Lord, teach us how to pray, as John also taught his disciples." Jesus complied literally with this request of his followers. As John, under the law, could only give rules and rudi- ments, not yet having come to the dispensation of grace and of the Spirit, so did Jesus give a form of prayer, a lesson in the "technique of worship." But only when he reaches the eve of his passion, when he announces the coming of the Comforter, does he lead his disciples into the heart and mys· tery of the great theme, teaching them to pray as John *could not* have taught his disciples. "Hitherto ye have asked nothing in my name," said Jesus, in his paschal discourse. But now that he was about to enter into his mediatorial office at God's right

hand, and to send forth the Comforter into the midst of his disciples, this joyful privilege was to be accorded to him : " Whatsoever ye shall ask the Father *in my name* he will give it you "[1] (John 16 : 23). The words are equivalent to *"in me."* The thought is not surely that of using the name of Jesus as a password or as a talisman, but of entering into his person and appropriating his will ; so that when we pray, it shall be as though Jesus himself stood in God's presence and made intercession. Nor is it "as though"—it is the literal fact. We become identified with Christ through the Spirit, now sent down, and his will is wrought within us by the Holy Ghost, so that to ask what we desire of him is to ask what he desires for us. We are inwilled by his will, because inspired by his Spirit, who lives and breathes within us. Therefore we may know that we are always heard, since we are in him who can boldly say to the Father : "I know that thou always hearest me." It is Christ's mediatorship with the Father, and the Holy Ghost's mediatorship with us, that gives us this high privilege of praying in the name of Jesus, as it is written : " For through him we both have access *in one Spirit* unto the Father."

When therefore, under the fuller development of

---

[1] It was impossible up to the time of the glorification of Jesus to pray to the Father in his name. It is a fullness of joy peculiar to the dispensation of the Spirit to be able to do so.—*Alford.*

doctrine as found in the epistles, we read of "pray-ing always with all prayer and supplication *in the Spirit*" (Eph. 6 : 18), and of "praying in the Holy Ghost" (Jude 20), it is simply an admonition to use our privilege of asking in the name of Jesus. For to be in the Spirit is to be in Christ, united to his person, identified with his will, invested with his righteousness, so that we are as he is before the Father.

In that fullest exposition of the doctrine of the Spirit, given in the eighth of Romans, we see clearly that the ministry of the Comforter consists in his effectuating in us that which Christ is accomplishing for us on the throne. Especially is this true of prayer. In the Epistle to the Hebrews we read : "Wherefore also he is able to save to the uttermost them that draw near to God through him, *seeing he ever liveth to make intercession for them*" (Heb. 7 : 25, R. V.). In the Epistle to the Romans we read : "And in like manner the Spirit also helpeth our infirmity; for we know not how to pray as we ought, but *the Spirit himself maketh intercession for us* with groanings which cannot be uttered; and he that searcheth the hearts know-eth what is the mind of the Spirit, because he maketh intercession for the saints according to the will of God" (Rom. 8 : 26, 27, R. V.). These passages, read together, clearly show the Spirit doing the same thing *in* us which Christ in heaven is doing *for* us. And, moreover, they reveal to us the method of the glorified Christ in helping those who know not what to pray for as they ought, teaching them, not by an outward form, but by an inward guidance. Indeed, the prayer inspired by the Holy Spirit is often so deep that it cannot be expressed in formal words, but reaches the ear of the Father only in unspeakable yearnings, in unuttered groanings. The keynote of all true intercession is the will of God. In the disciples' prayer, as taught them by the Master, this note is distinctly sounded: "Thy will be done on earth as in heaven." In the Saviour's garden-prayer it is heard again, as with strong crying and tears the Son of God exclaims: "Not my will but thine be done"; and in the revelation of the doctrine of prayer through an inspired apostle we read: "If we ask anything according to his will he heareth us." It is the Spirit's deepest work in the believer to attune his mind to this exalted key, as he "maketh intercession for the saints *according to the will of God.*" There is a promise which all disciples love to quote for their assurance in prayer: "If two of you shall agree on earth as touching anything that they shall ask, it shall be done for them of my Father which is in heaven" (Matt 18 : 19). The word translated "agree" is a very suggestive one. It is, συμφωνήσωσιν, from which our word "symphony" comes. If two shall *accord* or *symphonize* in what they ask, they have the promise of being heard. But, as in tuning an organ all the notes must be keyed to the standard pitch, else harmony were impossible, so in prayer. It is not enough that two disciples agree with each other; they must both accord with a Third—the righteous and holy Lord—before in the scriptural sense they can agree in intercession. There may be agreement which is in most sinful conflict with the divine will: " How is it that ye have agreed together [συνεφωνήθη, the same word] to tempt the Spirit of the Lord?" asks Peter (Acts 5 : 9). Here is mutual accord, but guilty discord with the Holy Ghost. On the contrary it is the Spirit's ministry to attune our wills to the Divine; thus only can there be praying in the Holy Ghost.

We cannot therefore emphasize too strongly the administration of the Spirit in directing the worship of God's house. The use of liturgical forms is a relapse into legalism, a consent to be taught to pray as " John taught his disciples." True, there may be extemporaneous forms as well as written forms, praying by rote as well as praying by the book. Against both habits we simply interpose the higher teaching of the Spirit, as belonging especially to this dispensation, in which the Father seeketh worshipers who " worship in Spirit and in truth." To pray rightly is the highest of all attainments. And it is so because the secret lies between these two opposites; a spirit supremely active while supremely passive, a heart prevailing with God because prevailed over by God. "O Lord," says a high saint, "my spirit was like a harp this morning, making melody before thee, since thou didst first tune the instrument by the Holy Spirit, and then didst choose the psalm of praise to be played thereon." Most solemn and suggestive words these have always seemed: "The Father seeketh such to worship him." Amid all the repetition of forms and the chanting of liturgies, how earnestly the Most High searches after the spiritual worshiper, with a heart inwardly retired before God, with a spirit so sensitive to the hidden motions of the Holy Ghost that when the lips speak they shall utter the effectual inwrought prayer that availeth much!

If any shall interpose the objection that what we are saying is too high to be practical, it may be well to confirm our position by the witness of· experience. We are not speaking of pulpit prayers especially, in what we have said. The universal priesthood of believers, which the Scriptures so plainly teach, constitutes the ground for common intercession, for "the praying one for another" which is the distinctive feature of the Spirit's dispensation. The prayer meeting, therefore, in which the whole body of believers participate, probably comes nearer the pattern of primitive Christian worship than any other service which we hold. To apply our principle here, then, what method is found most satisfactory? Shall the service be arranged beforehand, this one selected to pray, and that one to exhort; and during the progress of the worship, shall such a one be called up to lead the devotions, and such a one to follow? In a word, shall the service be mapped out in advance and manipulated according to the dictates of propriety and fitness as it goes on? One, after many years of experience, can bear emphatic testimony to the value of another way—that of magnifying the office of the Holy Spirit as the conductor of the service, and of so withholding the pressure of human hands in the assembly that the Spirit shall have the utmost freedom to move this one to pray and that one to witness, this one to sing and that one "to say amen at our giving of thanks," according to his own sovereign will. Here we speak not theoretically but experimentally. The fervor and spirituality and sweet naturalness of the latter method has been demonstrated beyond a peradventure, and that too, after an extended trial of both ways, the first in ignorance of a better way, with constant labor and worry and fret, and the last with inexpressible ease and comfort and spiritual refreshment. Honor the Holy Ghost as Master of assemblies; study much the secret of surrender to him; cultivate a quick ear for hearing his inward voice and a ready tongue for speaking his audible witness ; be submissive to keep silence when he forbids as well as to speak when he commands, and we shall learn how much better is God's way of conducting the worship of his house than man's way.[1]

(3) The service of song in the house of the Lord is another element of worship whose relation to the Spirit needs to be strongly emphasized. Spiritual singing has a divinely appointed place in the church of Christ. Church music, in the ordinary sense of that phrase, has no such place, but is a human invention which custom has, with many, unhappily elevated into an ordinance. We often quote the exhortation of the apostle : " Be filled with the Spirit," without marking the practical service with which this fullness stands immediately connected : " Speaking to yourselves in psalms and hymns and spiritual songs, singing and making melody in your heart to the Lord " (Eph. 5 : 19). As immediately as prayer is connected with the Holy Ghost in this same epistle : " Praying at all seasons *in the Spirit*", and our edification in the church : " Builded

---

[1] It were well for us to give more heed to the voice of Christian history as related to such questions as these. The rise of " sporadic sects " like the " Quietists," the " Mystics," the " Friends,'' and the " Brethren," with their emphasis on " the still voice " and " the inward leading,'' is very suggestive. If we may not go so far as some of these go in the insistence on speaking only as sensibly moved by the Spirit we may be admonished of the hard, artificial man-made worship which made their protest necessary.

together *in the Spirit*" (Eph. 2 : 22, R. V.); and our spiritual energizing: "Strengthened with power *through his Spirit*" (Eph. 3 : 16, R. V.); and our approach to God, "Access *in one Spirit* unto the Father" (2 : 18, R.V.), so intimately is the worship of praise here connected with the Holy Ghost and made dependent on his power.   Therefore it would seem too obvious to need arguing, that an unregenerate person is disqualified from ministering in the service of song in God's house.   Scripturally this seems incontestable; and as to the teaching of experience, we should hardly know how to name any custom which has brought a sorer blight upon the life of the church, or a heavier repression upon its spiritual energy, than the habit, now so general, of introducing unsanctified, unconverted, and even notoriously worldly persons into the choirs of the churches.

Now the teaching of the text just cited is decisive, not only against such performers in choirs, but against the choirs themselves, if by the latter term is meant certain ones employed to dispense music for the delectation of the congregation. For observe how distinctly the mutual and inter-congregational character of Christian singing is here pointed out : "Speaking *to one another* in psalms and hymns and spiritual songs." The one feature of the worship of the church, which distinguishes it radically and totally from that of the temple, is that it is mutual. Under the law there were priests and Levites to minister and people to be ministered to; under the gospel there is a universal spiritual priesthood, in which all minister and all are ministered to. Every act of service belonging to the Christian church is so described. There must be prayer, and the exhortation is, "Pray *one for another*" (James 5 : 16). There must be confession, and the injunction is : "Confess your sins *one to another*" (James 5 : 16, R. V.). There must be exhortation, and the command is : "Exhort *one another*" (Heb. 3 : 13). There must be love, and we are enjoined to "love *one another*" (1 Peter 1 : 22). There must be burden-bearing, and the exhortation is : "Bear ye *one another's* burdens" (Gal. 6 : 2). There must be comforting, and the command is : "Wherefore comfort *one another*" (1 Thess. 4 : 18). So with the worship of song. Its reciprocal character is emphasized, not only in the passage just quoted, but also in the Epistle to the Colossians : "Teaching and admonishing *one another* in psalms and hymns and spiritual songs" (Col. 3 : 16). This is according to the clearly defined method of the Spirit in this dispensation. He establishes our fellowship with the Head of the church, and through him with one another. All blessing in the body is mutual, and the worship which is ordained to maintain and increase that blessing· is likewise mutual.

As now the Spirit is the inspirer and director of the worship of God's church, he must have those who have been renewed and are indwelt by himself as the instruments through whom he acts; and by a teaching of Scripture too clear to be misunderstood all others are disqualified. How distinctly is this shown even in the types and symbols of the old dispensation. The holy anointing enjoined in Exodus for Aaron and his sons, is confessedly a type of the unction of the Holy Ghost. And mark the rigid and sacred limitations in its use: " And thou shalt anoint Aaron and his sons, and consecrate them that they may minister unto me in the priest's office. And thou shalt speak unto the children of Israel, saying: This shall be a holy anointing oil unto me throughout your generation. Upon man's flesh it shall not be poured; neither shall ye make any other like it, after the composition of it; it is holy, and shall be holy unto you; whosoever compoundeth any like it, or whoso putteth any of it upon a stranger, shall even be cut off from his people " (Exod. 30 : 30-33).

Now, of these minute directions and prescribed transactions we may say confidently that "they happened unto them for ensamples and they are written for our admonition, upon whom the ends of the world [ages] are come " (1 Cor. 10 : 11). The three rigid prohibitions here named touch just the errors which are most characteristic of the present generation. "*Upon man's flesh it shall not be poured*"; honoring the natural man, and exalting human nature into that place which belongs only to the regenerate. This is the error of those who believe in the universal sonship of the race, and call the carnal man divine. "*Whosoever putteth any of it upon a stranger.*" This is the sin of those who thrust into the ministry and service of the church persons who have never by the new birth through the Spirit been brought into the family of God, into the household of faith. "*Whosoever compoundeth any like it.*" This is the artificial imitation of the Spirit's offices and ministration. Let the Christian reader pause and ponder well this last prohibition. In the story of the primitive church sample sins are given for our warning, as well as specimen graces for our emulation. One such sin, so subtle, so dangerous, and so constantly recurring in Christian history, having taken the name of its first author and being called " simony," has been handed down from generation to generation. " Because thou hast thought that the gift of God can be purchased with money " is the solemn indictment against one who had purposed to buy the power of the Holy Ghost. Many desire the gifts of the Spirit who little care for the Spirit himself. Divine music is greatly coveted. Why not, with our thousands of gold, buy this spiritual luxury? Bring the singing men and singing women from the opera and from the concert hall; bid them compound a potion of sanctuary music, which shall entrance all ears and draw to the church those who could not be drawn thither by the plain attractions of the Cross. But what is the exhortation of Scripture? " By him therefore let us offer the sacrifice of praise to God continually, that is, the fruit of our lips, giving thanks to his name " (Heb. 13 : 15). This kind of sacrifice costs—earnest prayer, deep communion, and the fullness of the Spirit; but no sum of gold, however large, is adequate for its purchase, nor can any musician's art, however ingenious, imitate it.   Is there no approach to the sin of simony in those churches which spend thousands yearly in artistic music? And is not this attempted purchase of the Holy Ghost closely linked with the other sin of robbing God, considering how this lavish expenditure on artificial worship is almost always accompanied with meagre giving for the carrying out of the Great Commission? Our conclusion is, that the service of song has been committed to the church, and to the church alone, under the guidance of the Holy Spirit.   Some of her number may be appointed to lead this service, if they themselves are under the leadership of the Spirit. But the church cannot commit this divine ministry to unsanctified hireling minstrels, without affront to the Spirit of God and serious peril to her own communion with God.

If again any object that we are setting up an exaggerated and impossible ideal, let the voice of experience be heard in evidence. Let pastors be called to testify of the added blessing and fervor which have come to their sanctuaries when this ideal has been approximately realized. Let history repeat its story of song driven in times of apostasy into some narrow stall of the church, and into the hands of a few trained monopolists of worship; and then, in eras of revival, of the bursting of the barriers and the people of God seizing once more their defrauded heritage and breaking forth, a great multitude, into " hallelujahs of the heart." The annals of the Lollards, and of the Lutherans, and of the Wesleyans, and of the Salvationists bear harmonious witness on this point, and are deeply instructive.

3. *The Holy Spirit in the Missions of the Church.* In the Gospels which contain the story of Christ's earthly life we have the record of the giving of the Great Commission : " Go ye into all the world and preach the gospel to every creature." In the Acts, which contains the story of the life of the Spirit, we have the promise of the coming of the Executor of that Commission : " But ye shall receive power when the Holy Ghost is come upon you ; and ye shall be my witnesses, both in Jerusalem and in Judea and Samaria, and unto the uttermost part of the earth " (Acts 1 : 8, R. V.). Nowhere is the hand

of the Spirit more distinctly seen than in the origi-
nation and superintendence of missions. The field
is the world, the sower is the disciple, and the seed
is the word. The world can only be made ac-
cessible through the Spirit—"When he is come
he will convict the world of sin"; the sower is
energized only through the Spirit—"Ye shall receive the power of the Holy Ghost coming upon
you"; and the seed is only made productive
through the quickening of the Spirit—"He that
soweth unto the Spirit shall of the Spirit reap eternal life" (Gal. 6 : 8, R. V.). In the simple story of
the primitive mission, as recorded in the thirteenth
of Acts, we see how every step in the enterprise
was originated and directed by the presiding Spirit.
We observe this :

(1) In the selection of missionaries : "*The Holy
Ghost* said, Separate me Barnabas and Saul for
the work whereunto I have called them" (13 : 2).

(2) In their thrusting forth into the field : "So
they, being sent forth by the *Holy Ghost*, departed
unto Seleucia" (13 : 4).

(3) In empowering them to speak : "Then Saul,
who also is called Paul, filled with the *Holy Ghost*,
said" (13 : 9).

(4) In sustaining them in persecution : "And
the disciples were filled with joy and with the *Holy
Ghost*" (13 : 52).

(5) In setting the Divine seal upon their min-

istry among the Gentiles: "And God, which knoweth the hearts, bare them witness, giving *them the Holy Ghost*, even as he did unto us" (15 : 8).

(6) In counseling in difficult questions of missionary policy: "It seemed good *to the Holy Ghost and to us*" (15 ; 28).

(7) In restraining the missionaries from entering into fields not yet appointed by the Lord: They "were forbidden of the *Holy Ghost* to preach the gospel in Asia. . . They assayed to go into Bithynia but *the Spirit suffered them not*" (16 : 6, 7).

Very striking is this record of the ever-present, unfailing, and minute direction of the Holy Ghost in all the steps of this divine enterprise. "But this was in apostolic days," it will be said. Yes; but the promise of the Spirit is that "He shall abide with you for the age." Unless the age has ended he is still here, and still in office, and still entrusted with the responsibility of carrying out that work which is dearest to the heart of our glorified Lord. Who can say that there is not need in these days of a return to primitive methods and of a resumption of the Church's primitive endowments? The Holy Spirit is not straitened in himself, but only in us. If the Church had faith to lean less on human wisdom, to trust less in prudential methods, to administer less by mechanical rules, and to recognize once more the great fact that, having committed to her a supernatural work, she has appointed for her a supernatural power, who can doubt that the grinding and groaning of our cumbrous missionary machinery would be vastly lessened, and the demonstration of the Spirit be far more apparent?

VIII

THE INSPIRATION OF THE SPIRIT

"Have you visited the Cathedral of Freyburg, **and** listened to that wonderful organist, who with such enchantment draws the tears from the traveler's eyes while he touches, one after another, his wonderful keys, and makes you hear by turns the march of armies upon the beach, or the chanted prayer upon the lake during the tempest, or the voices of praise after it is calm? Well, thus the Eternal God, embracing at a glance the key-board of sixty centuries, touches by turns, with the fingers of his Spirit, the keys which he had chosen for the unity of his celestial hymn. He lays his left hand upon Enoch, the seventh from Adam, and his right hand on John, the humble and sublime prisoner of Patmos. From the one the strain is heard: 'Behold the Lord cometh with ten thousand of his saints'; from the other: 'Behold he cometh with clouds.' And between the notes of this hymn of three thousand years there is eternal harmony, and the angels stoop to listen, the elect of God are moved, and eternal life descends into men's souls." — *Gaussen's Theopneustia.*

VIII

THE INSPIRATION OF THE SPIRIT

INSPIRATION signifies inbreathing. Both the scribe and the Scripture, both the man of God and the word of God were divinely inbreathed. In that memorable meeting of the risen Lord and his disciples within the closed doors, we read that "*He breathed on them* and saith unto them, Receive ye the Holy Ghost; whosoever sins ye forgive, they are forgiven unto them; whosoever sins ye retain, they are retained" (John 20 : 22, R. V.). Well may the question of the scribes concerning Jesus now arise in our hearts concerning his disciples: "Who can forgive sins but God only?" And the answer should be: "True; God alone can forgive sins. And it is only because the Spirit of God, who is God, is in the apostles, endowing them with his divine prerogatives, that they are able to exercise this high authority."

We are persuaded, however, that this commission was not given to all Christians, though all have the Spirit. In a note in Olshausen's Commentary the matter seems to be correctly stated: "To the apostles was granted the power, absolute and unconditioned, of binding and loosing, just as to them was given the power of publishing truth unmixed with error. For *both* they possessed miraculous spiritual endowments." Only we should say "sovereign" rather than "miraculous" endowments. "*The Spirit breatheth where he wills*, and thou hearest his voice," said Jesus.[1] While miraculous gifts were not confined to the apostles, Christ may have committed to these, and to these alone, the sovereign prerogative of forgiving sins; gifts of healing, on the other hand, the working of miracles, prophecy, the discerning of spirits, and tongues, being distributed throughout the church; "but all these worketh one and the same Spirit, dividing to each one severally even *as he will*" (1 Cor. 12 : 11, R. V.). In a word, the action of the Holy Ghost was supremely sovereign in the assignment of spiritual offices, and when Jesus breathed on his apostles the Holy Ghost, and gave them authority

---

[1] John 3 : 8. "The wind bloweth where it listeth." Without pronouncing dogmatically, it must be said that the translation of Bengel and some others—"*The Spirit breatheth where he wills, and thou hearest his voice*"—has reasons in its favor which are well-nigh irresistible; *e. g.*, If τὸ πνεῦμα here is the *wind*, it has one meaning in the first part of the sentence and another meaning in the second; and that meaning too, one which it bears in no other instance of the more than two hundred and seventy uses of the word in the New Testament. It is not the word used in Acts 2 : 2, as might be expected if it signified wind. Then it seems unnatural to ascribe volition to the wind, θέλει. On the contrary, if the words apply to the Spirit, the saying is in entire harmony with other Scriptures, which affirm the sovereignty of the Holy Ghost in regeneration (John 1 : 13) and in the control and direction of those who are the subjects of the new birth (1 Cor. 12 : 4–11).

to remit sins, he separated them unto a prerogative of which others, indwelt by the same Spirit, might have known nothing.   It is very generally held that the order of apostles ceased with the death of those who had seen the Lord and companied with him until the day that he was received up.   But the reason for this cessation has been too little considered.   May we not believe that the apostles and their companions were commissioned to speak for the Lord until the New Testament Scriptures, his authoritative voice, should be completed?   If so, in the apostolate we have a provisional inspiration; in the gospel a stereotyped inspiration; the first being endowed with authority *ad interim* to remit sins, and the second having this authority *in perpetuam*.   The New Testament, as the very mouthpiece of the Lord, pronounces forgiveness upon all in every generation who truly repent and believe on the Son of God; and preachers in every age, with the Bible in their hand, are authorized to do the same declaratively.   But when it is urged, as by Catholic writers, that this infallibility for teaching and absolution, which was committed to the apostles, has descended through a succession of ministers called the clergy, the answer seems to be, that this authority has not been perpetuated in any body of men apart from the Scriptures, but was transferred to the New Testament and lodged there for all time.   Historically, at least, it seems to have been the fact, that as the apostles and prophets of the new dispensation disappeared, the Gospels and Epistles took their place, and that henceforth the divine authoritative voice of the Spirit could be distinctly recognized only in the written word. As coal has been called "fossil sunlight," so the New Testament may be called fossil inspiration, the supernatural illumination which fell upon the apostles being herein stored up for the use of the church throughout the ages.[1]

"All Scripture is given by inspiration of God [θεόπνευστος—God-breathed], and is profitable for doctrine, for reproof, for correction, for instruction in righteousness" (2 Tim. 3 : 16). As the Lord breathed the Spirit into certain men, and thereby committed to them his own prerogative of forgiving sin, so he breathed his Spirit into certain books and endowed them with his infallibility in teaching truth. God did not choose to inspire all good books, though he has chosen to

---

[1] The proof that the inspiration of the apostles and scribes of the New Testament was not transmitted to successors is thus stated by Neander: "A phenomenon singular in its kind is the striking difference between the writings of the apostles and those of the apostolic fathers, so nearly their contemporaries. In other instances transitions are wont to be gradual, but in this instance we observe a sudden change. There is no gentle gradation here, but all at once an abrupt transition from one style of language to another—a phenomenon which should lead us to acknowledge the fact of a special agency of the Divine Spirit in the souls of the apostles and of a new creative element in the first period."—*Church History*, II., 405.

inbreathe one book, thereby separating it and setting it apart from all other books.[1]   The phrase, "the Bible is simply literature," which some are using to-day, as a suggestion against bibliolatry, is not true.   Literature is the letter; Scripture is the letter inspired by the Spirit.   What Jesus said in justification of his doctrine of the new birth is equally applicable to the doctrine of inspiration: "That which is born of the flesh is flesh, and that which is born of the Spirit is spirit."   Educate, develop, and refine the natural man to the highest possible point, and yet he is not a spiritual man till, through the new birth, the Holy Ghost renews and indwells him.   So of literature; however elevated its tone, however lofty its thought, it is not Scripture.   Scripture is literature indwelt by the Spirit of God.   The absence of the Holy Ghost from any writing constitutes the impassable gulf between it and Scripture.   Our Lord, in speaking of his own doctrine, uses the same language, to show its separateness from common teaching which he employs above to mark the distinction of the new man.   He says: "It is the Spirit that quickeneth; the flesh profiteth nothing; *the words that I have spoken unto*

---

[1] There are the strongest reasons for rejecting the rendering of this passage as given in the Revised Version: "*Every Scripture inspired of God is also profitable*, etc.   The reader will find the objections to this rendering powerfully and conclusively set forth in Tregelles on Daniel.   Note, p. 267.

you are spirit and are life" (John 6 : 63, R. V.). Words they were, and in that respect, literature ; but words divinely inbreathed and therefore Scripture. In fine, the one fact which makes the word of God a unique book, standing apart in solitary separateness from all other writings, is that which also parts off the man of God from common men—the indwelling of the Holy Ghost. Therefore we may say truly of the Bible, not merely that it *was* inspired, but it *is* inspired ; that the Holy Ghost breathes within it, making it not only authoritative in its doctrine but life-giving in its substance, so that they who receive its promises by faith " have been begotten again, not of corruptible seed, but of incorruptible, through the word of God which liveth and abideth " (1 Peter 1 : 23, R. V.).

Thus far in this volume we have been dwelling upon the various works and offices of the Paraclete. Now we come to consider that the Holy Spirit not only acts but speaks. Let us listen to the repeated affirmations of this fact. Seven times our glorified Lord says, speaking in the Apocalypse : " He that hath an ear, let him hear what *the Spirit saith unto* the churches " (Rev. 2 : 7). The Paraclete on earth answers to the Paraclete above, so that to the voice from Heaven saying : " Write, blessed are the dead which die in the Lord from henceforth," the response is heard : " *Yea, saith the Spirit*, that they may rest from their labors," etc. (Rev. 14 : 13).

This accords with the general tenor of Scripture as to its own Author. In referring to the Old Testament, Peter says: "This Scripture must needs have been fulfilled, *which the Holy Ghost by the mouth of David spake before* concerning Judas, which was guide to them that took Jesus" (Acts 1 : 16). And again: "David himself *said by the Holy Ghost*" (Mark 12 : 36), our Lord thus plainly recognizing the voice of the Spirit in the voice of the psalmist. So again: "*The Spirit of the Lord spake by me*, and his word was in my tongue. The God of Israel said, the Rock of Israel spake to me" (2 Sam. 23 : 2, 3), and "Wherefore as *the Holy Ghost saith*, To-day if ye will hear his voice" (Heb. 3 : 7).

And what is it to speak? Is it not to express thought in language? The difference between thinking and saying is simply the difference of words. Therefore, if the Holy Ghost "*saith*," we are to find in the *words* of Scripture the exact substance of what he saith. Hence verbal inspiration seems absolutely essential for conveying to us the exact thought of God. And while many affect to ridicule the idea as mechanical and paltry, the conduct and method of scholars of every shade of belief show how generally it is accepted. For, why the minute study of the *words* of Scripture carried on by all expositors, their search after the precise shade of verbal significance, their attention to the minutest details of language, and to all the delicate coloring of mood and tense and accent? The high scholars who speak lightly of the theory of literal inspiration of the Scriptures by their method of study and exegesis are they who put the strongest affirmation on the doctrine which they deny. Then we cannot forget what we imply when we say that language is the expression of thought. Words determine the size and shape of ideas. As exactly as the coin answers to the die in which it is struck, does the thought answer to the word by which it is uttered. Vary the language by the slightest modification, and you by so much vary the thought.

As ultra spiritualism interprets Paul's words " *a spiritual body*," to mean a ghost, when the accent is as strongly on the σῶμα as on the πνευματικόν, his real thought evidently being that of a *body spiritualized;* so some, remembering that "the letter killeth," would etherealize Scripture by telling us that the divine idea is the chief thing, and the language quite secondary. But wisely and well has Martin Luther reminded us that " Christ did not say of his Spirit, but of his *words*, they are spirit and life."

To deny that it is the Holy Ghost who speaks in Scripture, is an intelligible position; but admitting that *he speaks*, we can only understand his thoughts by listening to his words. True, he may beget within us emotions too deep for expression, as when

"The Spirit himself maketh intercession for us with groanings which cannot be uttered" (Rom. 8 : 26). But the idea which is really intelligible is the idea that is embodied in speech. For finite minds, at least, words are the measure of comprehensible thoughts. Evidently Jesus claims for his teaching not only inspiration, but verbal inspiration, when he says that his *words* are "spirit and life." And to this agrees the saying of Paul, in speaking of the inspiration of the Holy Ghost : "But God hath revealed them unto us by his Spirit : for the Spirit searcheth all things, yea, the deep things of God. For what man knoweth the things of man, save the spirit of man which is in him? even so the things of God knoweth no man, but the Spirit of God. Now we have received, not the spirit of the world, but the Spirit which is of God, that we might know the things which are freely given to us of God, which things also we speak, *not in the words which man's wisdom teacheth, but which the Holy Ghost teacheth*, comparing spiritual things with spiritual " (1 Cor. 2 : 10–13).

And what if one objects that this theory makes inspiration purely mechanical, and turns the writers of Scripture into stenographers, whose office is simply to transcribe the words of the Spirit as they are dictated? It must be confessed that there is much in Scripture to support this view of the case. Should we see a student who, having taken down

the lecture of a profound philosopher, was now
studying diligently to comprehend the sense of the
discourse which he had written, we should understand simply that he was a pupil and not a master;
that he had nothing to do with originating either
the thoughts or the words of the lecture, but was
rather a disciple whose province it was to understand what he had transcribed, and so be able to
communicate it to others.   And who can deny that
this is the exact picture of what we have in the
following passage from Scripture : " Of which salvation the prophets have inquired and searched
diligently, who prophesied of the grace that should
come unto you, *searching what, or what manner of
time the Spirit of Christ which was in them did
signify, when it testified beforehand the sufferings of
Christ and the glory that should follow ;* unto whom
it was revealed," etc. (1 Peter 1 : 10, 11.) Here were
inspired writers, studying the meaning of what they
themselves had written. If they were prophets on
the manward side, they were evidently pupils on the
Godward side. With all possible allowance for the
human peculiarities of the writers, they must have
been reporters of what they heard, rather than the
formulators of that which they had been made to
understand. How nearly this also describes the
attitude of Christ,—a hearer that he might be a
teacher : " All things that I have heard of my
Father I have made known unto you " (John 15:

15); a reporter that he might be a revealer: "I have given unto them *the words* which thou gavest me" (John 17 : 8).

In these days scholars are very jealous for the human element in inspiration; but the sovereign element is what most impresses the diligent student of this subject. "The Spirit breatheth where he wills." Concerning regeneration by the Holy Ghost, we are carefully told that it is "not of the will of the flesh, nor *of the will of man*, but of God"; and concerning inspiration by the Spirit, the teaching is equally explicit: "For no prophecy ever came *by the will of man*, but men spake from God, being moved by the Holy Ghost" (2 Peter 1 : 21, R. V.).

The style of Scripture is, no doubt, according to the traits and idiosyncracies of the several writers, as the light within the cathedral takes on its various hues from passing through the stained windows; but to say that the thoughts of the Bible are from the Spirit, and the language from men, creates a dualism in revelation not easy to justify; so that we must quote with entire approval the words of an eminent writer upon this subject: "The opinion that the subject-matter alone of the Bible proceeded from the Holy Spirit, while its language was left to the unaided choice of the various writers, amounts to that fantastic notion which is the grand fallacy of many theories of inspiration; namely, that two spiritual agencies were in operation, one of which produced the phraseology in the outward form, while the other created within the soul the conceptions and thoughts of which such phraseology was the expression. The Holy Spirit, on the contrary, as the productive *principle*, embraces the entire activity of those whom he inspires, rendering their language the *word of God*." [1]

If it be urged that the quotations which the New Testament makes from the Old are rarely *ipsissima verba*, the language being in many instances greatly changed, it should be noted in reply how significant even these changes often are. If the Holy Spirit directed in the writing of both books, he would have a sovereign right to alter the phraseology, if need be, from the one to the other. In the opinion of many scholars the change of "the Redeemer shall come *to* Zion, and unto them that turn from transgression in Jacob," in Isa. 59 : 20, to "There shall come *out* of Zion the Deliverer," in Rom. 11 : 26, is an inspired and intentional change.[2] So of the citation from Amos 9 : 11, "In that day will I raise up the tabernacle that is fallen," as given in Acts 15 : 16, "After these things I will return, and I will build again the tabernacle of David which is fallen "; the modification of the language seems designed, in order to make clear its significance in its present setting. Many other examples might be given of

---

[1] Lee on the " Inspiration of the Holy Scripture," pp. 32, 33.

[2] See Lange's " Commentary " *in loco*.

a reshaping of his own words by the divine Author of Scripture.   On the other hand, the constant recurrence of the same words and phrases in books of the Bible most widely separated in the time and circumstances of their composition, strongly suggests identity of authorship amid the variety of penmanship.   The individuality of the writers was no doubt preserved, only that their individuality was subordinated to the sovereign individuality of the Holy Spirit.   It is with the written word as with the incarnate Word.   Because Christ is divine, he is more truly human than any whom the world has ever seen ; and because the Bible is supernatural, it is natural as no other book which was ever written ; its divinity lifts it above those faults of style which are the fruits of self-consciousness and ambition. Whether we read the Old Testament story of Abraham's servant seeking a bride for Isaac, or the New Testament narrative of the walk of the risen Christ with his disciples to Emmaus, the inimitable simplicity of the diction would make us think that we were listening to the dialect of the angels who never sinned in thought, and therefore cannot sin in style, did we not know rather that it is the phraseology of the Holy Spirit.[1]

---

[1] I am satisfied only with the style of Scripture.   My own style and the style of all other men cannot satisfy me.   If I read only three or four verses I am sure of their divinity on account of their inimitableness.   *It is the style of the heavenly court.*—*Oetinger.*

An eminent German theologian has written a sentence so profoundly significant that we here reproduce it in Italics : " *We can in fact speak with good reason of a language of the Holy Ghost. For it lies in the Bible plainly before our eyes, how the Divine Spirit, who is the agent of revelation, has fashioned for himself a quite peculiar religious dialect out of the speech of that people which forms its theatre.*"[1] So true do we hold this saying to be, that it seems to us quite impossible that the exact meaning of many of the terms of the New Testament Greek should be found in a Lexicon of classic Greek. Though the verbal form is the same in both, the inbreathed spirit may have imparted such new significance to old words, that to employ a secular dictionary for translating the sacred oracles, were almost like calling an unregenerate man to interpret the mysteries of the regenerate life. Do we not know how modern progress and discovery have even put new meanings into many English words, so that one must be in "the spirit of the age" in order to comprehend them?[2] Thus like-

---

[1] Rcthe, " Dogmatics," p. 238.

[2] For example, Shakespeare, and Milton, and Dryden, employ the words " car" and " engine" and "train" in their writings ; but living before the age of steam and railways they knew nothing of the meaning which these terms convey to us. And it is possible that Homer and Plato knew as little of the meaning of such words as αιών and παράκλητος, as found in the revelation of Jesus Christ, by whom " the ages were framed " and the Comforter sent down.

wise, even in the work of verbal criticism, it is essential that one possess the spirit of Christ in order to translate the words of Christ.

As to the question of the "inerrancy of Scripture," as the modern phrase is, we may well pass by many minor arguments, and emphasize the one great reason for holding this view, viz.: If it is God the Holy Ghost who speaks in Scripture, then the Bible is the word of God, and like God, infallible. A recent brilliant writer has challenged us to show where the Bible anywhere calls itself "The word of God." [1] The most elementary student of the subject can, with the aid of a concordance, easily point out the passages which so describe it. But we dwell on the fact that is not only called ὁ λόγος τοῦ θεοῦ, "the word of God," but τὰ λόγια τοῦ θεοῦ, "the oracles of God." This collective name of the Scriptures is most significant. We need not inquire of the heathen as to the meaning which they put upon the words as the authoritative utterances of their gods; let the usage of Scripture make its own impression: "What advantage then hath the Jew? or what is the profit of circumcision? Much every way; first of all, that they were intrusted with the oracles of God" (Rom. 3 : 2, R. V.).[2]

This comprehensive expression is very helpful

---

[1] Dr. R. F. Horton, in "Verbum Dei."

[2] The apostle in calling the Old Testament Scriptures the "ora cles of God," clearly recognizes them as divinely inspired books. The

to our faith. When critics are assailing the books of the Old Testament in detail, the Holy Spirit authenticates them for us in their entirety. As Abigail prayed for a soul "bound in the bundle of life" with the Lord, so here an apostle gives us the books of the Law and the Prophets and the Psalms bound together in one bundle of inspired authority. Stephen, in like manner, speaks of his nation as "those who received the *lively oracles* (of God) to give unto us" (Acts 7 : 38); and Peter says, "If any man speak let him speak as *the oracles of God*" (1 Peter 4 : 11). And not only this; the same apostles who submitted to the authority of the Old Testament as the oracles of God, themselves claimed to write as the oracles of God in the New Testament. "If any man," says Paul, "think himself to be a prophet or spiritual, let him acknowledge that the things that I write unto you are the *commandments of the Lord*" (1 Cor. 14 : 37). "We are of God," writes John. "He that knoweth God heareth us; he that is not of God heareth not us" (1 John 4 : 16). These claims are too great to be put forth concerning fallible writings. Admitting their premises, the Jews were right in charging Jesus with blasphemy, in that being a man

---

Jewish church was the trustee and guardian of these oracles till the coming of Christ. Now the Scriptures of the Old and New Testament are committed to the guardianship of the Christian Church.— *Dr. Philip Schaff.*

he made himself God.   If Christ is not God, he is
not even a good man.   And if the Scriptures are
not inerrant, they are worse than errant; since,
being literature, they make themselves the word of
God.

And what if it be said that there are irreconcila-
ble contradictions in this book which calls itself the
oracles of God?   Two things may be said: First,
it should be expected that under "the scientific
method" such contradictions should appear and
constantly multiply.   The Bible is a sensitive plant,
which shuts itself up at the touch of mere critical
investigation.   In the same paragraph in which it
claims that its very words are the words of the Holy
Spirit, it repudiates the scientific method as futile
for the understanding of those words: "Eye hath
not seen, nor ear heard,"—and insists on the spiritual method as alone adequate,—"but God hath
revealed them unto us by his Spirit" (1 Cor. 2:
9, 10).   Not only does the Bible not yield roses to
the critic, it yields the thorns and briars of hopeless
contradiction.   "*Intellige ut credas verbum meum,*"
said Augustine to the rationalists of his day, "*sed
crede ut intelligas verbum Dei.*"   "Understand
my word, that you may believe it; believe God's
word, that you may understand it."   Faith holds
not only the keys of all the creeds, but of all
the contradictions.   He who starts out and proceeds under the conviction that the Bible is the

infallible word of God, will find discrepancies constantly turning into unisons under his study.   And
this remark leads to the second observation : that
the contradictions of man may really be the harmo-
nies of God.   An uncultivated listener, hearing an
oratorio of one of the great masters, would detect
discords again and again in the strains ; and as a
matter of fact, what are called "accidentals" in
music are discords, but discords inserted to
heighten the harmony.   Thus, as one after another
of the alleged discrepancies of Scripture having
been noted and made to jar upon the ear have
then been reconciled, with what an emphatic and
heightened harmony have the words of the psalmist, speaking by the Holy Ghost, fallen on our ear :
" The law of the Lord is perfect, converting the
soul ; the testimony of the Lord is sure, making
wise the simple " !   There seems to the critic to be
historic error in the statement of Stephen that
Jacob was buried at Sychem (Acts 7 : 16) instead of in the field of Machpelah before Mamre,
as recorded in Gen. 50 : 13, just as it was once
thought that Luke had made a mistake, not to
be explained away, in his reference to Cyrenius
in chapter 2 : 1, 2.   But as the latter contradiction
has disappeared, only confirming the veracity of
Scripture by the investigation which it has called
forth, so may the former.   And so also with such
alleged discrepancies as that between the record in

one place that King Solomon had four thousand stalls for horses, and in another forty thousand ; or that of the statement in one passage that King Josias began to reign at eight years of age, and in another, at eighteen.   What if we freely admit that we cannot reconcile these statements ?   That does not prove that they are not reconcilable.   The history of solved contradictions has certainly shown this, that as "the foolishness of God is wiser than men, and the weakness of God stronger than men," so the discords of God are more harmonious than men.

We may say, in closing this chapter, that almost the highest proof of the infallibility of Scripture is the practical one, that we have proved it so ; that as the coin of the State has always been found able to buy the amount represented on its face, so the prophecies and the promises of Holy Scripture have yielded their face value to those who have taken pains to prove them.   If they have not always done so, it is probable that they have not yet matured. Certainly there are multitudes of Christians who have so far proved the veracity of Scripture that they are ready to trust it without reserve in all that it pledges for the world yet unseen and the life yet unrealized.   "Believe that thou mayest know," then, is the admonition which Scripture and history combine to enforce.   In the farewell of that rare saint, Adolph Monod, these golden words occur :

"When I shall enter the invisible world, I do not expect to find things different from what the word of God represented them to me here. The voice I shall then hear will be the same I now hear upon the earth, and I shall say, 'This is indeed what God said to me; *and how thankful I am that I did not wait till I had seen in order to believe.*'"

IX

THE CONVICTION OF THE SPIRIT

" The Comforter in every part of his threefold work glorifies Christ. In convincing of sin he convinces us of the sin of not believing on Christ. In convincing us of righteousness, he convinces us of the righteousness of Christ, of that righteousness which was made manifest in Christ going to the Father, and which he received to bestow on all such as should believe in him. And lastly, in convincing of judgment, he convinces us that the prince of the World was judged in the life and by the death of Christ. Thus throughout, Christ is glorified ; and that which the Comforter shows to us relates in all its parts to the life and work of the incarnate Son of God."—*Julius Charles Hare.*

IX

THE CONVICTION OF THE SPIRIT

" AND when he is come *he will convict the world in respect of sin, and of righteousness, and of judgment*" (John 16 : 8, R.V.). It is too large a conclusion which many seem to draw from these words, that since the day of Pentecost the Spirit has been universally diffused in the world, touching hearts everywhere, among Christians and heathen, among the evangelized and the unevangelized alike, and awakening in them a sense of sin. Does not our Lord say in this same discourse concerning the Comforter : " *Whom the world cannot receive*, because it seeth him not neither knoweth him " ? (John 14 : 17.) With these words should be associated the limitation which Jesus makes in the gift of the Paraclete : " If I depart I will send him *unto you.*" Christ's disciples were to be the recipients and distributors of the Holy Ghost, and his church the mediator between the Spirit and the world. " And when he is come (to you) he will reprove the world." And to complete the exposition, we may connect this promise with the Great Commission, " Go ye into *all the world* and preach the gospel to every creature," and conclude that when the

Lord sends his messengers into the world, the Spirit of truth goes with them, witnessing to the message which they bear, convincing of the sin which they reprove, and revealing the righteousness which they proclaim. We are not clear to affirm that the conviction of the Spirit here promised goes beyond the church's evangelizing, though there is every reason to believe that it invariably accompanies the faithful preaching of the word.

It will help us then to a clear conception of the subject, if we consider the Spirit of truth as sent *unto the church*, testifying *of Christ*, and bringing conviction *to the world.*

As there is a threefold work of Christ, as prophet, priest, and king, so there is a threefold conviction of the Spirit answering thereto : " And he, when he is come, will convict the world in respect of sin and of righteousness and of judgment ; of sin, because they believe not on me ; of righteousness, because I go to the Father and ye behold me no more ; of judgment, because the prince of this world hath been judged" (John 16 : 8–12, R. V.). It is concerning the testimony of Christ as he spake to men in the days of his flesh ; and concerning the work of Christ now carried on in his intercession at God's right hand ; and concerning the sentence of Christ when he shall come again to be our judge, that this witness of the Spirit has to do.

" *He shall convince the world of sin.*"   Why is he

needed for this conviction since conscience is present in every human breast, and is doing his work so faithfully? We reply: Conscience is the witness to the law; the Spirit is the witness to grace. Conscience brings legal conviction; the Spirit brings evangelical conviction; the one begets a conviction unto despair, the other a conviction unto hope.

"*Of sin, because they believe not on me*," describes the ground of the Holy Spirit's conviction. The entrance of Christ into the world rendered possible a sin hitherto unknown: "If I had not come and spoken unto them, they had not had sin; but now they have no cloak for their sin" (John 15 : 22). Evil seems to have required the presence of incarnate goodness, in order to its fullest manifestation. Hence the deep significance of the prophecy spoken over the cradle of Jesus: "Behold this child is set for the fall and rising again of many in Israel; and for a sign which shall be spoken against, *that the thoughts of many hearts may be revealed*" (Luke 2 : 34, 35). All the most hideous sins of human nature came out during the betrayal and trial and passion of our Lord. In that "hour and power of darkness" these sins seem indeed to have been but imperfectly recognized. But when the day of Pentecost had come, with its awful revealing light of the Spirit of truth, then there was great contrition in Jerusalem—a contrition the sting of which we find in the charge of Peter: "Jesus of Nazareth, whom ye have taken and by wicked hands have crucified and slain." Was not that deep conviction, following the gift of the Spirit, in which three thousand were brought to repentance in a single day, a conviction of sin because they had not believed on Christ?

For our reproof the Holy Ghost presents another side of the same fact, calling us to repentance, not for having taken part in crucifying Christ, but for having refused to take part in Christ crucified; not for having been guilty of delivering him up to death, but for having refused to believe in him who was "delivered for our offenses and raised again for our justification." Wherever, by the preaching of the gospel, the fact of Christ having died for the sins of the world is made known, this guilt becomes possible. The sin of disbelieving on Christ is, therefore, the great sin now, because it summarizes all other sins. He bore for us the penalties of the law; and thus our obligation, which was originally to the law, is transferred to him. To refuse faith in him, therefore, is to repudiate the claims of the law which he fulfilled and to repudiate the debt of infinite love which, by his sacrifice, we have incurred. Nevertheless, the Spirit of truth brings home this sin against the Lord, not to condemn the world, but that the world through him might be saved. In a word, as has been well said, "it is not the sin-question but the Son-question" which we really raise now in preaching the gospel. "Christ having perfectly satisfied God about sin, the question now between God and your heart is: Are you perfectly satisfied with Christ as the alone portion of your soul? Christ has settled every other to the glory of God." In dealing with the guilty Jews, it was the historical fact which the Holy Ghost urged for their conviction: "Ye denied the Holy One and the Just, and killed the Prince of Life" (Acts 3 : 14, 15). In dealing with us Gentiles, it is rather the theological or evangelical fact: "Christ also hath once suffered for sins, the just for the unjust, that he might bring us to God" (1 Peter 3 : 18), and you are condemned that you have not believed on him and confessed him as Saviour and Lord. It is the same sin in the last instance, but viewed upon its reverse side, if we may say it. In the one case it is the guilt of despising and rejecting the Son of God ; in the other, it is the guilt of not believing in him who was despised and rejected of men. Yet if submissively yielded to, the Spirit will lead us from this first stage of revelation to the second, since what Andrew Fuller said of the doctrines of theology is equally true of the convictions of the Spirit, that "they are united together like chain-shot, so that whichever one enters the heart the other must certainly follow."

"*Of righteousness, because I go to the Father and*

ye see me no more."   Not until he had been seated in the heavenly places had Christ perfected righteousness for us.   As he was "delivered for our offenses and raised again for our justification," so must he be enthroned for our assurance.   It is necessary to see Jesus standing at the right hand of God, in order to know ourselves "accepted in the Beloved."   How beautiful the culmination of Isaiah's passion-prophecy wherein, accompanying the promise that "he shall bear the sin of many," is the prediction that "by his knowledge *shall my righteous servant justify many*"!   But he must be shown to be righteous, in order that he may justify; and this is what his exaltation does.   "It was the proof that him whom the world condemned, God justified—that the stone which the builders rejected, God made the Headstone of the corner— that him whom the world denied and lifted up on a cross of shame in the midst of two thieves, God accepted and lifted up in the midst of the throne."[1]

The words "and because ye see me no more," which have perplexed the commentators, seem to us

[1] For as the ministry of Enoch was sealed by his reception into heaven, and as the ministry of Elijah was also abundantly proved by his translation, so also the righteousness and innocence of Christ. But it was necessary that the ascension of Christ should be more fully attested, because upon his righteousness, so fully proved by his ascension, we must depend for all our righteousness. For if God had not approved him after his resurrection, and he had not taken his seat at his right hand, we could by no means be accepted of God.—*Cartwright.*

to give the real clue to the meaning of the whole passage. So long as the High Priest was within the veil, and unseen, the congregation of Israel could not be sure of their acceptance. Hence the eager anxiety with which they waited his coming out, with the assurance that God had received the propitiation offered on their behalf. Christ, our great High Priest, has entered into the Holy of Holies by his own blood. Until he comes forth again at his second advent, how can we be assured that his sacrifice for us is accepted? We could not be, unless he had sent out one from his presence to make known this fact to us. And this is precisely what he has done in the gift of the Holy Ghost. "Who being the brightness of his glory, and the express image of his person, and upholding all things by the word of his power, when he had by himself purged our sins, he sat down on the right hand of the Majesty on high" (Heb. 1 : 3). There he will remain throughout the whole duration of the great day of atonement, which extends from ascension to advent. But in order that his church may have immediate assurance of acceptance with the Father, through his righteous servant, he sends forth the Paraclete to certify the fact ; and the presence of the Spirit in the midst of the church is proof positive of the presence of Jesus in the midst of the throne; as is said by Peter on the day of Pentecost : " Therefore being by the right hand of God exalted, and having received of the Father the promise of the Holy Ghost, he hath shed forth this which ye now see and hear " (Acts 2 : 33).

Now the Lord's words seem plain to us.   Because he ascends to the Father, to be seen no more until his second coming, the Spirit meantime comes down to attest his presence and approval with the Father as the perfectly righteous One.   How clearly this comes out in Peter's defense before the Council :   "The God of our fathers raised up Jesus, whom ye slew and hanged on a tree.   Him hath God exalted with his right hand to be a Prince and a Saviour, for to give repentance to Israel and forgiveness of sins ; and we are witnesses of these things, *and so also is the Holy Ghost*, whom God hath given to them that obey him " (Acts 5 : 30–32). Why this two-fold witness ?   The reason is obvious.   The disciples could bear testimony to the crucifixion and resurrection of Christ, but not to his enthronement ; that event was beyond the ken of human vision ; and so the Holy Ghost, who had been cognizant of that fact in heaven, must be sent down as a joint-witness with the apostles, that thus the whole circle of redemption-truth might be attested.   Therein was the promise of Jesus in his last discourse literally fulfilled :   " But when the Comforter is come, whom I will send unto you from the Father, even the Spirit of truth which proceedeth from the Father, he shall testify of me; and ye also shall bear witness, because ye have been with me from the beginning" (John 15 : 26, 27).

As we have said, it is not only the enthronement of Christ in righteous approval with the Father that must be certified, but the acceptance of his sacrificial work as a full and satisfying ground of our reconciliation with the Father. And the Spirit proceeding from God is alone competent to bear to us this assurance. Therefore in the Epistle to the Hebrews, after the reiterated statement of our Lord's exaltation at the right hand of God, it is added: "For by one offering he hath perfected forever them that are sanctified, *whereof the Holy Ghost is also a witness to us*" (Heb. 10 : 14, 15). In a word, he whom we have known on the cross as "the Lamb of God that taketh away the sins of the world," must now be known to us on the throne as "*the Lord our righteousness*." But though the angels and the glorified in heaven see Jesus, once crucified, now "made both Lord and Christ," we see him not. Therefore it is written that "no man can say Jesus is Lord, *but in the Holy Spirit*" (1 Cor. 12 : 3, R. V.). So also we are told that "if any man sin we have a *Paraclete* with the Father, Jesus Christ the righteous" (1 John 2 : 1) ; but we can only know Christ as such through that "other Paraclete" sent forth from the Father. It was promised that "when he, the Spirit of truth, is come, he shall not speak from himself; but what things soever he shall hear, these shall he speak" (John 16 : 13, R.V.). Hearing the ascriptions of worthiness lifted up to Christ in heaven, and beholding him who was made a little lower than the angels for the suffering of death, now "crowned with glory and honor," he communicates what he sees and hears to the church on earth.   Thus, as he in his earthly life, through his own outshining and self-evidencing perfection, "was justified in the spirit"; so we, recognizing him standing for us in glory, and now "of God made unto us righteousness," are also "justified in the name of the Lord Jesus *and by the Spirit of our God*" (1 Cor. 6 : 11).

Thus, though unseen by the church during all the time of his high-priestly ministry, our Lord has sent to his church one whose office it is to bear witness to all he is and all he is doing while in heaven, that so we may have "boldness and access with confidence by the faith of him," and that so we may come boldly to the throne of grace, "the Holy Ghost this signifying"—what he could not under the old covenant—"that the way into the holiest of all" (Heb. 9 : 8) has been made manifest.

And yet—strange paradox—in this identical discourse in which Jesus speaks to his disciples of seeing him no more, he says: "Yet a little while and the world seeth me no more, *but ye see me;* because I live ye shall live also" (John 14 : 19); words which by common consent refer to the same time of Christ's continuance within the veil.   But it is now by the inward vision, which the world has not, that they are to behold him.   And they are to behold him *for the world*, since Christ said of him: "Whom the *world cannot receive, because* it seeth him not, neither knoweth him."   And yet it is "to *convince the world*" "of sin and of righteousness and of judgment" that the Spirit was to be sent.   How shall we make it plain?   When the sun retires beyond the horizon at night, the world, our hemisphere, sees him no more; yet the moon sees him, and all night long catches his light and throws it down upon us.   So the world sees not Christ in the gracious provisions of redemption which he holds for us in heaven, but through the illumination of the Comforter the church sees him; as it is written: "Eye hath not seen, nor ear heard, neither have entered into the heart of man the things which God hath prepared for them that love him; *but God hath revealed them unto us by his Spirit*" (1 Cor. 2 : 9, 10).   And the Church seeing these things, communicates what she sees to the world.   Christ is all and in all; and the Spirit receives and reflects him to the world through his people.

> The moon above, the church below,
>   A wondrous race they run;
> But all their radiance, all their glow,
>   Each borrows of its sun.

"*Of judgment, because the prince of this world is judged.*" Here, we believe, is a still farther advance in the revelation of the gospel, and not a retreat to the doctrine of a future judgment, as some would teach. For we repeat our conviction, that in this entire discourse the Holy Spirit is revealed to us as an evangel of Grace, and not as a sheriff of the Law. Hear the Apostle Peter once more, as, pointing to him who had been raised from the dead and seated in the heavenlies, he says: "By him every one that believeth is justified from all things from which ye could not be justified by the law of Moses" (Acts 13 : 39, R. V.). Justification, in the evangelical sense, is but another name for judgment prejudged and condemnation ended. In the enthroned Christ every question about sin is answered, and every claim of a violated law is absolutely met ; and though there is no abatement in the demands of the decalogue, yet because "Christ has become the end of the law for righteousness to every one that believeth," now "*grace reigns through righteousness* unto eternal life by Jesus Christ our Lord." Strange paradox set forth in Isaiah's passion psalm : "*By his stripes we are healed*," as though it were told us that sin's smiting had procured sin's remission. And so it is. If the Holy Spirit shows us the wounds of the dying Christ for condemning us, he immediately shows us the wounds of the exalted Christ for comforting us.

His glorified body is death's certificate of discharge, the law's receipt in full, assuring us that all the penalties of transgression have been endured, and the Sin-bearer acquitted.

The meaning of this last conviction seems plain therefore: "*Of judgment, because the prince of this world is judged.*" Recall the words of Jesus as he stood face to face with the cross: "Now is the judgment of this world; now shall the prince of this world be cast out" (John 12 : 31). "The accuser of the brethren" is at last non-suited and ejected from court. The death of Christ is the death of death, and of the author of death also. "That through death he might destroy him that hath the power of death, that is, the devil; and deliver them who, through fear of death, were all their lifetime subject to bondage" (Heb. 2 : 14, 15). If the relation of Satan to our judgment and condemnation is mysterious, this much is clear, from this and several passages, that Christ by his cross has delivered us from his dominion. We must believe that Jesus spoke the literal truth when he said: "Verily, verily, I say unto you, he that heareth my word and believeth him that sent me, hath eternal life, *and cometh not into judgment*, but hath passed out of death into life" (John 5 : 24, R. V.). On the cross Christ judged sin and acquitted those who believe on him; and in heaven he defends them against every re-arrest by a violated law.

"There is therefore now no condemnation to them that are in Christ Jesus" (Rom. 8 : 1). Thus the threefold conviction brings the sinner the three stages of Christ's redemptive work, past judgment and past condemnation into eternal acceptance with the Father.

In striking antithesis with all this, we have an instance in the Acts of the threefold conviction of conscience, when Paul before Felix "reasoned of *righteousness, and temperance, and the judgment to come*" (Acts 24 : 25). Here the sin of a profligate life was laid bare as the apostle discoursed of chastity; the claims of righteousness were vindicated, and the certainty of coming judgment exhibited; and with the only effect that "Felix trembled." So it must ever be under the convictions of conscience, —compunction but not peace. We have also an instructive contrast exhibited in Scripture, between the co-witness of the Spirit and the co-witness of conscience. "*The Spirit himself beareth witness* (συμμαρτυρεῖ) that we are the children of God" (Rom. 8 : 16). Here is the assurance of sonship, with all the divine inward persuasion of freedom from condemnation which it carries. On the other hand is the conviction of the heathen, who have only the law written in their hearts: "*Their conscience bearing witness* (συμμαρτυρούσης), their thoughts one with another accusing, or else excusing them, in the day when God shall judge the secrets of men" (Rom.

2 : 15, 16). Conscience can "accuse," and how universally it does so, abundant testimony of Christian missionaries shows; and conscience can "excuse," which is the method that guilty thoughts invariably suggest; but *conscience cannot justify*. Only the Spirit of truth, whom the Father hath sent forth into the world, can do this. The work of the two witnesses may be thus set in contrast:

Conscience Convinces—	*The Comforter Convinces—*
Of sin committed;	Of sin committed;
Of righteousness impossible;	Of righteousness imputed;
Of judgment impending.	Of judgment accomplished.

Happily these two witnesses may be harmonized, as they are by that atonement which reconciles man to himself, as well as reconciles man to God. Very significantly does the Epistle to the Hebrews, in inviting our approach to God make, as the condition of that approach, the "having our hearts *sprinkled from an evil conscience*." As the High Priest carried the blood into the Holy of Holies in connection with the old dispensation, so does the Spirit take the blood of Christ into the inner sanctuary of our spirit in the more wondrous economy of the new dispensation, in order that he may "cleanse your conscience from dead works to serve the living God" (Heb. 9 : 14). Blessed is the man who is thus made at one with himself while made at one with God, so that he can say: "I say the truth in Christ, I lie not, *my conscience also bear-*

ing me witness in the Holy Ghost " (Rom. 9 : 11).
The believer's conscience dwelling in the Spirit,
even as his life is "hid with Christ in God," both
having the same mind and bearing the same testimony—this is the end of redemption and this is
the victory of the atoning blood.

X

THE ASCENT OF THE SPIRIT

" The Apostle Paul evidently saw the redemption of the bodies of the saints and their manifestation as the sons of God and with them the redemption of the whole creation from its present bondage to be the complete harvest of the Spirit, whereof the church doth now possess only the first-fruits, that is, the first ripe grains which could be formed into a sheaf and presented in the temple as a wave-offering unto the Lord. 'That Holy Spirit of Promise which is the earnest of our inheritance,' saith the same apostle—the earnest, like the first-fruit, being only a part of that which is to be earned. . . yet a sufficient surety that the whole shall in the fullness of the times, be likewise ours."—*Edward Irving.*

X

THE ASCENT OF THE SPIRIT

"HE that descended is the same also that ascended up far above all heavens." So writes the apostle concerning the Paraclete who is now with the Father, "Jesus Christ the righteous" (Eph. 4 : 9). And what is true of the one is true of that "other Paraclete," the Holy Ghost, who was sent down to abide with us during this age. When he has accomplished his temporal mission in the world he will return to heaven in the body which he has fashioned for himself—that "one new man," the regenerate church, gathered out from both Jews and Gentiles during this dispensation. For what is the rapture of the saints predicted by the apostle when, at the sound of the trumpet and the resurrection of the righteous dead, "we which are alive and remain shall be caught up together with them in the clouds to meet the Lord in the air"? (1 Thess. 4 : 17.) It is the earthly Christ rising to meet the heavenly Christ; the elect church, gathered in the Spirit and named ὁ χριστός, (1 Cor. 12 : 12,) taken up to be united in glory with "Christ, the Head of the church, himself the Saviour of the body" (Eph.

5 : 23, R. V.).   In the council at Jerusalem this is announced as the distinctive work of the Spirit in this
dispensation "to gather out *a people for his name.*"
It was not by accident and as a term of derision
that the first believers received their name; but
"the disciples were divinely called *Christians* first
in Antioch" (Acts 11 : 26).   This was the name
pre-ordained for them, that "honorable name" by
which they are called (James 2 : 7).   When, therefore, this out-gathering shall have been accomplished, and *the people for his name* shall be completed, they will be translated to be one with him
in glory, as they were one with him in name, the
Head taking the body to himself, "as Christ also,
the church" (Eph. 5 : 29).   And this translation of
the church is to be effected by the Holy Spirit who
dwells in her.   "But if the Spirit of him that
raised up Jesus from the dead dwell in you, he that
raised up Christ from the dead shall also quicken
your mortal bodies by his Spirit that dwelleth in
you (Rom. 8 : 11).   It is not by acting upon the
body of Christ from without, but by energizing it
from within, that the Holy Ghost will effect its
glorification.   In a word, the Comforter, who on
the day of Pentecost, came down to form a body
out of flesh, will at the *Parousia* return to heaven
in that body, having fashioned it like unto the body
of Christ, that it may be presented to him "not
having spot, or wrinkle, or any such thing, . . holy

and without blemish" (Eph. 5 : 27). Is it meant to be implied in what is here said that the Comforter is to leave the world at the time of the advent, to return no more? By no means. And yet what is meant needs to be very explicitly set forth.

A very able writer on the doctrine of the Spirit makes this remark, so striking and yet so true that we have put it in italics : *"As Christ shall ultimately give up his kingdom to the Father* (1 Cor. 15 : 24–28), *so the Holy Ghost shall give up his administration to the Son, when he comes in glory and all his holy angels with him."* [1] The church and the kingdom are not identical terms, if we mean by the kingdom the visible reign and government of Jesus Christ on earth. In another sense they are identical. As the King, so the kingdom. The King is present now in the world, only invisibly and by the Holy Spirit ; so the kingdom is now present invisibly and spiritually in the hearts of believers. The King is to come again visibly and gloriously ; so shall the kingdom appear visibly and gloriously. In other words, the kingdom is already here in mystery : it is to be here in manifestation. Now the spiritual kingdom is administered by the Holy Ghost, and it extends from Pentecost to *Parousia.* At the *Parousia*—the appearing of the Son of Man in glory—when he shall take unto himself his great power and reign (Rev. 11 : 17), when he who has

---

1 "Through the Eternal Spirit," by Elder Cumming, D. D., p. 185.

now gone into a far country, to be invested with a kingdom, shall return and enter upon his government (Luke 19 : 15), then the invisible shall give way to the visible; the kingdom in mystery shall emerge into the kingdom in manifestation, and the Holy Spirit's administration shall yield to that of Christ.

Here our discussion properly ends, since the age-ministry of the Holy Spirit terminates with the return of Jesus Christ in glory. But there is an "age to come" (Heb. 6 : 5), succeeding "the present evil age" (Gal. 1 : 4), and we may, in closing, take a glimpse at that for the light which it may throw upon the present dispensation.

What significance has the phrase, "*the first-fruits of the Spirit*," which several times occurs in the New Testament? The first-fruits is but a handful compared with the whole harvest; and this is what we have in the gift of "the Holy Spirit of promise, *which is the earnest of our inheritance until the redemption of the purchased possession*" (Eph. 1 : 13, 14). The harvest, to which all the first-fruits look forward, is at the appearing of the Lord. Christ, by his rising from the dead, became "*the first-fruits of them that slept*" (1 Cor. 15 : 20). The full harvest, of course, is at the advent, when "they that are Christ's at his coming" shall be raised up (1 Cor. 15 : 23). So of the Holy Ghost. We have all the Spirit, but *not all of the Spirit*. As a person of the God-head, he is here in his entirety; but as to his ministry, we have as yet but a part or earnest of his full blessing. To make this statement plain, let us observe that the work of the Holy Spirit, during this entire dispensation, is elective. He gathers from Jew and Gentile the body of Christ, the *ecclesia*, the called-out. This is his peculiar work in this gospel age. In a word, the present is the age of election, and not of universal ingathering.

But is this all we have to hope for? Let the word of God answer. Paul, in considering the hope of Israel, says that there is at this present time "*a remnant according to the election of grace*"; and a little farther on he declares that in connection with the coming of the Deliverer "*all Israel shall be saved*" (Rom. 11 : 5, 26). Here is an elective out-gathering, and then a universal in-gathering; or, as the apostle sums it up in this same chapter: "*If the first-fruits be holy, so also the lump.*" On the other hand, James, speaking by the Holy Ghost concerning the Gentiles, says first that "God did visit the Gentiles *to take out of them a people for his name,*" and "after this will I return," etc., "that the residue of men might seek after the Lord, and *all the Gentiles upon whom my name is called, saith the Lord*" (Acts 15 : 14, 17). Here, again, is first an elective out-gathering and then a total in-gathering.

Now, by looking at other scriptures, it seems clear that the Holy Spirit is the divine agent in both these redemptions, the partial and the total. If we refer to Joel's great prophecy : "*I will pour out my Spirit upon all flesh,*" and then to Peter's reference to the same, as recorded in the Acts, we are led to ask, Was this prediction completely fulfilled on the day of Pentecost ? Clearly not. Peter, with inspired accuracy, says : "*This is that which was spoken by the prophet Joel,*" without affirming that herein the prophecy of Joel was entirely fulfilled. Turning back to the prediction itself, we find that it includes within its sweep "the great and the terrible day of the Lord," and the "bringing again of the captivity of Judah and Jerusalem" (Joel 2 : 31 ; 3 : 1), events which are clearly yet future. If again we examine the vivid prophecy of Israel's conversion, we observe that their looking upon him whom they pierced, and mourning for him, follows the prediction : "And I will pour upon the house of David, and upon the inhabitants of Jerualem the Spirit of grace and supplication" (Zech. 12 : 10). So in the picture of the desolations of Jerusalem, as they have actually existed during the present age, the prophet represents this judgment of thorns and briars and forsaken palaces and desertion of population, as continuing "*until the Spirit be poured upon us from on high*" (Isaiah 32 : 15).

Indeed the Scriptures seem to be harmonious in

their teaching that, after the present elective work of the Spirit has been completed, there will come a time of universal blessing, when the Spirit shall literally be "poured out upon all flesh"; when "that which is perfect shall come" and "that which is in part shall be done away."

Thus in the doctrine of the Spirit there is a constant reference to the final consummation. "The Holy Spirit of God, in whom ye were sealed *unto the day of redemption*," says Paul (Eph. 4 : 30). Again : "Ourselves also which have the first-fruits of the Spirit, even we ourselves, groan within ourselves, waiting for the adoption, to wit, *the redemption of our body*" (Rom. 8 : 23).

All which the Comforter has yet brought us, or can now bring us, is only the first sheaf of the great harvest of redemption which awaits us on our Lord's return. "Ye have received *the Spirit of adoption*, whereby we cry Abba, Father" (Rom. 8 : 15); but for the adoption itself we wait; sons of God already by birth from above, we with the whole creation yet wait for "*the manifestation of the sons of God*" (Rom. 8 : 19).

To his tender exhortation to be patient until the coming of the Lord, which James writes in the fifth chapter of his epistle, there is added the suggestive illustration : "Behold the husbandman waiteth for the precious fruit of the earth, being patient over it until it receive the early and latter rain."

As in husbandry the one rain belonged to the time of sowing, and the other to the time of harvest, so in redemption the early rain of the Spirit was at Pentecost, the latter rain will be at the Parousia; the one fell upon the world as the first sowers went forth into the world to sow, the other will accompany "the harvest which is the end of the age," and will fructify the earth for the final blessing of the age to come, bringing repentance to Israel and the remission of sins, "that the times of refreshing may come from the presence of the Lord, and that he may send Jesus Christ, before appointed for you, whom the heavens must receive until the times of the restitution of all things" (Acts 3 : 19–21).

SCRIPTURE INDEX

GENERAL INDEX